STATE OF DISREPAIR

The Hoover Institution gratefully acknowledges

THE EWING MARION KAUFFMAN FOUNDATION

for their significant support of this publication.

STATE OF DISREPAIR

Fixing the Culture and Practices
of the State Department

Kori N. Schake

HOOVER INSTITUTION PRESS

STANFORD UNIVERSITY   STANFORD, CALIFORNIA

The Hoover Institution on War, Revolution and Peace, founded at Stanford University in 1919 by Herbert Hoover, who went on to become the thirty-first president of the United States, is an interdisciplinary research center for advanced study on domestic and international affairs. The views expressed in its publications are entirely those of the authors and do not necessarily reflect the views of the staff, officers, or Board of Overseers of the Hoover Institution.

www.hoover.org

Hoover Institution Press Publication No. 620

Hoover Institution at Leland Stanford Junior University,
Stanford, California 94305-6010

Hoover Institution Press assumes no responsibility for the persistence or
accuracy of URLs for external or third-party Internet websites referred
to in this publication, and does not guarantee that any content on such
websites is, or will remain, accurate or appropriate.

First printing 2012
18 17 16 15 14 13 12   7 6 5 4 3 2 1

Manufactured in the United States of America

The paper used in this publication meets the minimum Requirements of
the American National Standard for Information Sciences—Permanence
of Paper for Printed Library Materials, ANSI/NISO Z39.48-1992. ⊚

Cataloging-in-Publication Data is available from the Library of Congress.

ISBN: 978-0-8179-1454-7 (cloth. : alk. paper)
ISBN: 978-0-8179-1456-1 (e-book)

"All diplomacy is war by other means."

Zhou Enlai

CONTENTS

FOREWORD

I first met Kori last year at a dinner honoring Stanford students who either are currently serving or have served in the military. In a casual conversation I learned both of her deep interest and expertise in the military and foreign policy (she's on the faculty of the United States Military Academy at West Point and has served as deputy director of the Policy Planning Staff). I also learned that she had recently completed this book—a book that, in part, talks about how the State Department might better accomplish its mission by learning something from the military. It is a provocative and apt comparison. It also raises profound and important questions about leadership and organizational change.

I indicated to Kori that although I had no expertise in the State Department (other than a one-month assignment when I was in the Army), organizational change was a topic that I did know something about. For the past thirty years I have studied and consulted with organizations ranging from private-sector corporations to international agencies and public institutions as they have attempted to transform themselves, sometimes successfully and sometimes not. Her book sounded fascinating because, at its heart, it proposes how the State Department—a critically important organization for America—needs to fundamentally transform itself. I asked if I might read a draft of her book.

In reading the book, I was struck at her practical wisdom and insight into the problems and challenges facing the leaders of the State Department. Although leaders of public-sector organizations often claim how "unique" their challenges are, my experience refutes that. Of course there are special circumstances involved in managing within the public sector—but there are special challenges in leading almost any organization. As I read Kori's description of the responsibilities confronting the leaders of the State Department, I was struck at how similar those problems are to other large-scale change efforts. In my view, this was good news in that we know what it takes to successfully transform organizations, and those lessons can help the leaders of the State Department.

Kori drives home this message in her discussion of how the U.S. military has been able to transform itself and how those hard-earned lessons might help the State Department. Indeed, many of the lessons learned by leaders such as Carlos Ghosn (who transformed Nissan), Lou Gerstner (who saved IBM), Gordon Bethune (who took Continental Airlines from worst to first among U.S. airlines), or Dan Vasella (who took a mediocre pharmaceutical company and transformed it into a world leader) apply directly to the transformation Kori proposes. Some within the State Department will be offended by comparing their hallowed organization to the crass likes of an airline or a car company. They will claim (defensively) that the challenges they face are different. But, after reading her book, I believe that this is not true. The difference between the State Department and other organizations is that the mission of the State Department *is* more important than that of airlines and computer companies, which means that the responsibilities of its leaders are also greater. If a private-sector firm misses its financial goals, shareholders may lose some money. If the leaders of the State Department fail in their mission, the United States suffers.

This book offers a compelling and practical case for how leaders in the State Department can make their organization better and more effective. Written in a highly accessible way and filled with practical advice and concrete examples, it is a book that is broadly relevant for managers and organizational scholars as well as members of government.

In an important way, this is a book about leadership and organizational change. Kori's recommendations deserve to be taken seriously and acted on by leaders in our government. If they fail at this, they will have failed as leaders—and failed the American people whom they claim to serve.

PROFESSOR CHARLES A. O'REILLY III
Frank E. Buck Professor of Management
Hank McKinnell-Pfizer Director of the Center
for Leadership Development and Research
Graduate School of Business
Stanford University

ACKNOWLEDGMENTS

I am deeply grateful to Carl Schramm, that tornado of Schumpeterian creative destruction, for encouraging me to write this book. Among his many fine qualities is his encouragement of ideas he doesn't agree with—under his stewardship of the Ewing Marion Kauffman Foundation has become a major generator of ideas. I can't say often enough, and never without smiling, how much I appreciate the Kauffman Foundation funding work it knew to be arguing against the position it advocated on expeditionary economics. It is so indicative of the foundation's commitment to the power of ideas that it supports its critics in a belief that is how ideas are tested and how better solutions, where there may be better solutions, are developed.

The Hoover Institution continues to be my ideal employer; what else needs be said about a leadership team that cultivates ideas to advance a free society and practices as management the institution's guiding philosophy? Thank you, John Raisian, Dave Brady, and Stephen Langlois.

This book benefited greatly from my experience working in the Pentagon, in the State Department, and on the National Security Council. I hadn't realized before working in the Joint

Staff that American military leaders are great teachers. They live in an environment in which they can't be successful without making everyone around them successful, and I was a beneficiary of that teaching in ways that continue to shape my professional development.

The culture shock of working in the Department of State for someone who'd professionally grown up in the Pentagon is difficult to overstate. While State's defenders argue its functions necessitate a different culture and mode of operations, it is difficult to maintain that the institution assists rather than impedes the success of its mission. For me, the most striking difference was the willingness in military culture to turn a hard critical eye on its failings and correct them; at State there is a greater tendency to explain the difficulties of doing what they do better. It is a culture of description, not problem-solving.

Working in coalition management from 2002–2005 on the National Security Council brought the difficulty of "whole-of-government operations" starkly to life. The Office of the Secretary of Defense was often an aggravating impediment to carrying out the president's policies, but the State Department's incapacity was a much bigger problem. Simply stated, the United States government was—and I believe still is—incapable of whole-of-government operations because the civilian agencies (especially the Department of State) are too weak to perform the necessary functions.

Those functions have been migrating to the Pentagon because they cannot wait. The deficiencies of interagency performance in the Bush administration were unique, but they have not abated in the subsequent administration. These are not principally problems of personality; they are deeply entrenched problems of institutional performance. Ten years into the wars, the military has adapted and improved its performance remarkably; the State Department hardly at all.

In fact, State's incapacity has created the impression that it cannot provide the basis for development assistance or other crucial civilian functions on which success of our arms in the wars depends. That is why Carl Schramm and so many others are convinced the military needs to take over a broader swath of inherently civilian activity in war zones. I believe that is not a good enough answer. It penalizes the military for being good at its work while not requiring State to become so.

I am especially grateful to former Secretary of State Condoleezza Rice, who was extraordinarily generous with her insights on the State Department during her tenure. Ambassador Eric Edelman gave me a master class on the Foreign Service and its culture and proved himself a virtuoso diplomat when I overstayed my welcome. Former directors of Policy Planning Steve Krasner and David Gordon turned their formidable analytic minds to the question of why State doesn't add more value to the policymaking process. Professor Charles O'Reilly of the Stanford Graduate School of Business was an enthusiastic spur to my understanding about the parallels of State's difficulties with other organizations struggling to be successful.

Numerous other colleagues with experience with the departments of State and Defense have generously shared their thinking with me. Some are cited in annotation; many preferred to add their ideas into the mix of my thinking without attribution. All helped me think through the nature of the problem and identify potential solutions because they share the view that the country needs, and the people of the State Department deserve, an institution that takes their professionalism seriously and sets them up to be successful.

CHAPTER 1

Introduction

This book grows out of a project by the Kauffman Foundation exploring an idea called expeditionary economics. The generator of that idea, Dr. Carl Schramm, believes the community of development experts is profoundly mistaken about how to foster economic growth.[1] He argues that the mistakes of development professionals are impeding the war effort in Iraq and Afghanistan, because in both wars our strategy is contingent on building stable and prosperous democratic governments. And he recommends adding economic development as a core competency of the American military in order to solve this problem.

I agree with most of the expeditionary economics argument: development professionals have a poor record of engendering actual economic development; spurring economic growth in the counterinsurgency wars we are fighting is essential to succeeding in those wars; and our civilian agencies are not achieving what we need in order to capitalize on our military gains and win the wars.

I differ with the expeditionary economics argument over whether the American military ought to become the institution that undertakes development work, though. The United States government already has an agency entirely dedicated to assisting countries with economic development: the U.S. Agency for International Development (USAID). The departments of State, Agriculture, Treasury, and Justice, and many other civilian agencies, have important roles to play in helping create the political and legal environment, transportation and banking infrastructure, and market information that will facilitate development in Iraq, Afghanistan, and other places where the American military is operating.

Instead of tasking the American military with yet another inherently civilian function, I believe work should focus on bringing those agencies of the government whose job it is to provide development assistance up to the standard of success that expeditionary economics identifies as necessary for the success of our war efforts. This is both a practical bias—as I doubt the military will prove adept at economic development due to competing priorities—and a fervent moral belief that when our country puts Soldiers, Sailors, Airmen and Marines into harm's way, we owe them competent counterparts in their civilian agencies.[2]

Those agencies, or at least the majority of them, have not proved competent partners to our military in Iraq and Afghanistan. We simply do not hold them to the same standard of performance as we hold our military. As a result, the military has of necessity taken on roles that divert its attention from its central tasks and for which it is neither ideally suited nor ideally seen as the conveyer of American government policies. Rather than make the American military good at development work, we need to make the other elements of our government that are engaged in winning the war as good at their jobs as is the American military.

Principal among those agencies is the Department of State, which has statutory responsibility for U.S. government activity abroad. No agency has been more ambitious than State in envisioning a leading role for itself, yet no agency has been more disappointing in its contribution. This book seeks to explain what about the institutional culture and current practices of the Department of State cause it to fall so far short of both the leading role it aspires to and the objective needs of American strategy for winning the wars we are fighting. Its suggestions are offered with an earnest desire to support both the mission and the good people of the Department of State. They deserve, as our military deserves, the tools and institutional processes that set them up for success.

CHAPTER 2

Nature of the Problem

The most conventional of conventional wisdom in Washington in the past five years is that the U.S. State Department is dramatically undernourished for the work required of American civilian power. Since 2000, there have been a staggering number of think tank reports advocating a more robust diplomatic corps. The last three secretaries of state and the last two directors of the U.S. Agency for International Development have not only had ambitious goals for improving their departments, they have actually implemented at least the resourcing of them: Congress has increased funding by 155 percent since 2003 and the size of the diplomatic corps has grown by 50 percent.

There has emerged strong support for "whole-of-government operations," by which is meant the coordinated use of all elements of state power. The Obama administration has dedicated itself to practicing "smart power," a further polishing of the concept, emphasizing a rebalancing of governmental effort away from dependence on military force and toward diplomatic and economic levers. Inside the Beltway, whole-of-government operations and smart power are the holy grail, much yearned for yet elusive.

Earnest advocates of effective American engagement in the world envision the military's role returning to small proportions as other government agencies, principally the State Department, increase their influence and activity.

Yet there is practically no one who believes the State Department is currently performing at a level adequate to the need. There are no voices arguing the State Department is a diplomatic equivalent to the dominance displayed by the American military, none who think America's diplomats stand astride the world like a colossus. Our diplomats punch below their weight and carry less influence than our country's power ought to deliver. Even sympathetic observers conclude that "today's Foreign Service does not have to a sufficient degree the knowledge, skills, abilities, and outlooks needed to equip career diplomats to conduct 21st-century diplomacy."[1] Despite the substantial increase in the workforce at State, it continues to contract out work that is mission-critical or whose function is inherently governmental.[2]

State has a better record than it gets credit for, certainly. It established twenty new embassies in Europe after 1991 without additional personnel, and the diplomats who have joined the Foreign Service since 2001 are much more likely to want to deploy to Provincial Reconstruction Teams in Iraq or Afghanistan and to change the world for the better, rather than remain safely ensconced in embassies and report on changes as they occur.

Still, the Department of State underperforms, both for what the country needs and for the resources it has. Foggy Bottom chants the mantra of whole-of-government operations but remains—even by Secretary of State Hillary Clinton's own assessment—inadequate to the task.[3]

If further proof were needed, it would be that major swaths of activity that are civilian in nature continue to migrate to the military. The militarization of American foreign policy does not reflect an ambition by the military; it reflects the vacuum left by inadequate civilian power. Work needs doing, and the Department of State remains incapable of doing it. The most recent example would be governance issues in Afghanistan: small unit military leaders, rather than diplomats, are working to create local councils throughout the country. The military command has established a high-level anti-corruption task force and is setting up legal and judicial structures—both functions that ought to be civilian activities. Despite the existence of an embassy of over a thousand civilians in Kabul, those tasks have not been undertaken by civilians.[4]

The inability of State to improve is not for lack of ideas or effort at the highest echelons of the department. Typically, secretaries of state invest little in the professionalization of the department. Instead, they spend all their time on policies rather than the functioning of the institution. But the last three secretaries of state developed major initiatives to improve the performance of the department: Secretary Colin Powell's Diplomatic Readiness Initiative, Secretary Condoleezza Rice's Transformational Diplomacy, and Secretary Hillary Clinton's Diplomacy 3.0. In all three cases, the leadership teams identified shortcomings, developed policies to redress the shortcomings, and were successful in gaining funding support for their initiatives. What none of them proved successful at has been substantially affecting the culture of the State Department such that it responded to their priorities.

There are no more fervent advocates of a more vibrant American diplomacy than the American military. Former Defense Secretary Robert Gates and former Chairman of the Joint Chiefs of Staff Admiral Michael Mullen have been the apostles of greater State Department funding, routinely advocating for it publicly, to the Congress, and within government counsels. They have not declined additional Defense spending in favor of diplomatic funding, or offered more than what would be considered a trivial amount of money in the defense budget to achieve that improved

State Department (roughly $100 million in the defense budget has a dual key for spending on activities that State and Defense jointly agree need doing). But they have gone further than any other DOD leadership in supporting increased spending for diplomacy. Both Gates and Mullen testified with the secretary of state to State's Authorizing and Appropriating Committees of the Congress in support of greater funding.[5]

Bringing the Pentagon's sensibilities to the problems of improving American diplomacy sheds light on why State has not been more successful. The Department of State is deficient in three crucial areas in which the Department of Defense excels: mission focus, education, and programming. Adopting DOD attitudes and commitments to these areas may prove more valuable to State than any additional money DOD leaders could help attain.

The American military exists to fight and win our nation's wars; everything else is subordinated to that essential task. Moreover, it is the function American taxpayers and their representatives in Congress value, and demand of, our military. The Department of State has no equivalent focus. To the extent the institution can identify its priorities, what State values about American diplomacy is engagement in multinational negotiation and reporting on international activity. These are the functions that shape the culture of the Department; they are not, however, the functions of greatest value outside the institution.

Protecting Americans at home and abroad through excellence in consular service should be the primary function of America's diplomats: preventing dangerous enemies from attaining visas to travel to the United States, ensuring Americans traveling overseas have the protection of our government, encouraging educational and other involvement with talented foreigners. These are the bread and butter—what prospectors would call the grub stake—of diplomacy, the activities that can only be performed by diplomats but on the success of which all Americans rely.

Yet they are the activities least valued by the Department of State: consular service is the lowest priority "cone," or specialization, in the Foreign Service. Talented diplomats are not tracked into that branch. It is as though the Army and Marine Corps did not consider ground combat their principal function. This needs to change if the State Department is to build a strong institutional base as the lead agency for American foreign policy. State needs to clearly embrace consular activity as its essential function and realign the incentives and thereby the culture of the institution. Doing so would bring the State Department significant advantages, both in the operation of the organization and in its support by the public and Congress.

The people of the State Department are among the American government's most talented. They come into the diplomatic corps with, on average, a graduate education and eleven years of work before joining the Foreign Service. State's personnel policies utilize the skills developed before entry into the service; they do not build skills. Hiring needed skills rather than developing them isn't a bad strategy, but it hinges crucially on identifying skills the institution needs and recruiting them. By its own admission, State is not hiring the skills it identifies as essential.

The Department of State compounds the error of not recruiting the skills it needs by not investing in the kind of professional education and training that will make our diplomats successful for the demands they face as their careers progress. The people who are successful in the State Department are people who can be thrown in the deep end of the swimming pool and not drown; but the department never teaches them to swim, and the successful ones even come to discredit the value of swimming lessons, because they succeeded without them.

State has twice in the past seven years been authorized increases in staffing levels in order to build time into diplomats' careers for education and training: Secretary Powell's Diplomatic

Readiness Initiative in 2003 and Secretary Rice's Transformational Diplomacy Initiative in 2006. More recently, Secretary Clinton has also requested and received additional Foreign Service and civil service positions. Yet none of these substantial increases of people resulted in American diplomats receiving appreciably more professional education and training, or building time into their career tracks to participate in it. Training remains either a voluntary (off-duty) activity or something the department's most valuable people are not freed up to participate in. Secretary Powell made mandatory some valuable leadership training, but there has been no major effort to develop a core curriculum of knowledge that diplomats need at different thresholds in their careers or to develop a process by which diplomats are rewarded for undertaking it.

It merits mention that even the most starry-eyed believers in leading through civilian power assess the cost to produce it to be minimal. They are not arguing to double or triple the budget, they are arguing for marginal annual increases. One of the most functionally ambitious and carefully accounted studies of increased funding puts the sticker price of achieving sufficiency at only $3.3 billion across four years.[6] Such a sum is roughly a 1.5 percent increase per year over the $52.8 billion current spending for operations of the department, a small number even before comparison to the $525 billion baseline budget request of the Defense Department for the coming year.[7] *Think of it: 1.5 percent per year for four years.*

Two conclusions leap out from this fact: first, that it would take pathetically little to invest at the level diplomatic experts consider fully funding their needs; and second, that if they believe their performance can be so vastly improved on such a thin margin of additional resourcing, they probably have very little idea what it would take to actually make themselves a successful organization.

It is tempting just to give State all the money it could imagine (for the years of chronic underfunding have badly diminished its ability to even imagine truly ambitious horizons) and hold it accountable for producing the dramatic improvements in performance its advocates believe are just barely out of reach. But the Department of State lacks the rigorous culture of program analysis and evaluation that exists in the Department of Defense, and which provides DOD a much stronger basis for advancing and defending its spending requests within the executive branch and to Congress. It is arguable that the second most powerful person in the Department of Defense is not the Chairman of the Joint Chiefs of Staff, but the comptroller, who develops and defends the budget. Until 2009, the Department of State didn't even have a parallel figure; it still lacks the analytic offices undergirding DOD's comptroller.

It is perverse that the chronic underfunding of the Department of State (and there isn't even a faction of policy analysts that argue State has been adequately funded since the end of the cold war) created a vague budgetary culture. One would think that resource demands competing for limited funds would foster careful husbandry and transparent accounting. Just the opposite is true. State has a terrible reputation on Capitol Hill for pulling rabbits out of its budgetary hat instead of carefully costing and tracking programs in ways that would build congressional confidence in its ability to manage larger budgets. For State to achieve the kinds of sustained budget increases that advocates of stronger civilian power seek, it will need to develop a long-term budget perspective and the ability to prioritize its activity to make better use of the resources it gets.

This book is an attempt to illustrate how deficiencies in focus, education, and programmatic proficiency impede the work of the State Department and to demonstrate how investing in those areas could in the space of just a few years produce American diplomats who genuinely are the peers of their military counterparts and who can undertake with a high level of skill the work at which our country urgently needs them to be successful. It presents a vision of what a successful State Department looks like and seeks to build support for creating that State Department. The means are actually largely in the State Department's authorities; very little legislation or funding would be needed from Congress to bring about the change.

The militarization of American foreign policy is bad for our country. We can and should strengthen our civilian power. But the State Department has not proven capable of identifying and redressing its inadequacies. The recent Quadrennial Diplomacy and Development Review (QDDR) claims to pose the question, "How can we do better?" but its answer can be summed up as, "By having more money and more senior positions." Yet resources cannot wholly be the answer, given the influx of money State has received in the past decade.

State must develop the means of assessing activity so that it can make a credible case that money spent on civilian power is a better investment than the alternatives. Asserting leadership has not worked; it must be earned by demonstrating the intellectual and operational proficiencies that will draw adherents. Credibility begins with demonstrating excellence and asking for it to be rewarded once achieved. Instead of surveying its own ranks (as the QDDR did), State should throw itself open to the kind of consumer satisfaction surveys that would inform its priorities and resourcing. It would learn an awful lot from interagency partners, recipients of both civilian and military engagement, aid organizations, and other stakeholders.

Imagine a State Department that actually does lead American foreign policy, one whose ideas for shaping the world in positive ways drive the agenda of America's engagement and build a broad basis of public support to which elected leaders would respond. Imagine a State Department whose data drive public and congressional analyses of problems and programs and whose diplomats are so expert that they are foreign and domestic journalists' preferred interviews and major universities' preferred hires. Imagine a department that is a magnet for entrepreneurial people of diverse skills and which puts those skills to creative use, fostering professional growth, with employees whose ability is so obvious that they are pulled by other agencies and constantly at risk of being poached by the private sector so that State has to fight to keep them. Imagine a department in which competition for retention is so fierce that it drives a personnel pyramid wide at the base, with an educational program so rigorous it equips our diplomats to succeed at every level of their career and draws applicants from the military and foreign countries to learn what our diplomats know. And imagine a department with personnel policies that identify emergent needs and encourage activity rather than description; one whose senior leadership is so proficient and commands activity so expansive that the Pentagon would seek to place four-star generals as deputies to diplomats rather than give diplomats consolatory slots in our military headquarters.

We should not just imagine such a State Department. We should demand it. And we know how to achieve these things; we do it in our military. Businesses all across the country achieve it. We just don't bother to do it in our civilian agencies on which the success of our military efforts depends. The suggestions in this book are offered in the earnest hope that the State Department and the Obama administration will seize the moment and create a more solid basis for civilian-led American diplomacy. The country deserves it, and the good people of the State Department deserve it, too.

CHAPTER 3

Atrophy of Diplomatic Power

If asked, "How can you do better?" the Department of State's corporate reaction would be, "We are so much better than you give us credit for." This attitude permeates the recent Quadrennial Diplomacy and Development Review.[1] The organization has a defensive mentality, reacting to any criticism as unfair. Even State's leadership tends to conflate criticism of performance with lack of support for the mission or the people of the department.

Secretary Rice describes it as "Pentagon envy."[2] The members of the Department of State believe they deserve the respect accorded to the military and resent the fact that they do not have the enduring popularity of the American military with the public and with the Congress. Our military historically leads by a significant margin in Gallup polls of the institution most admired and trusted in American society, leading organized religion, the presidency, and even the Supreme Court.[3] The defensive attitude at State springs from a belief that the department does work which is equally dangerous and difficult, but never is accorded the admiration or the support that accrues to the military.

The conclusion is accurate: State is not viewed with the respect, or given the resources, provided to the military. Deputy Secretary of State Richard Armitage humorously described the congressional attitude toward the Foreign Service, saying, "Foreign policy is not an exotic rite practiced by an ordained priesthood."[4]

Diplomats explain the variance on the basis that "there is no constituency for foreign policy." And it is true that few Americans have direct experience with our diplomats; in a country of 313 million people, only 2 million a year seek consular assistance overseas.[5] But it does not follow that there is no constituency for diplomacy; the State Department simply does not invest in building a constituency for itself in the way the military services do.

Protecting State from criticism does not make the department stronger, nor does cheerleading that isn't founded on real successes. Successful organizations are organizations that critique their own operations harshly and learn to improve. Business writing is replete with paeans to the value of this approach, such as Intel founder Andy Grove's *Only the Paranoid Survive*. The American Army improved significantly in the 1980s when the practice of after-action reviews became more ruthless and national training centers were established to put units through testing at which they were expected to fail in order to better determine why they failed and so strengthen their weaknesses.[6]

The Golden Age

There is a tendency among State partisans to yearn for the mythic glory days of American diplomacy, when gods walked the earth as diplomats and negotiation was the paramount tool of state power. This golden age is variously thought to be the era of the Founding Fathers or World War II and its aftermath. Such a gilded assessment would have come as a surprise to the practitioners of American diplomacy in both those periods.

John Adams considered his diplomatic service the low point of his life and was so despondent on his first posting to Paris he even ceased writing his wife, the only significant breach of their long correspondence. He reviled the decadence and corruption of the French court and of the American legation associated with it (and which turned out to be not only engaged in financial corruption but also penetrated by British spying).[7] Adams may have been ill-suited for a diplomat, especially in the *louche* ancien régime setting of Paris, but he was by no means a man to undervalue his achievement. While in the Netherlands he secured crucial loans to fund the war; while in Britain he mollified King George's attitude toward his former colony.

Benjamin Franklin and Thomas Jefferson more richly enjoyed their tours of duty representing the new republic to French society, and Franklin achieved an enormous good by bringing French diplomatic support, armed forces, and financing to the American revolution. Both ministers reveled in the valuable function of representing a cultured and intellectual America to societies tending (rightly) to consider the new republic rough. These are storied successes, but we remember them perhaps more so for the men who achieved them than for the achievements themselves. Louis XV did not extend French aid to America out of appreciation of Franklin or Jefferson, but as a means to advance France's interests by impeding Britain.

Which gets us to the fundamental difference between force and diplomacy: military force compels outcomes that by definition the adversary opposes; diplomacy cajoles an adversary into acting as though it wants what we want. Diplomacy often claims success by statecraft at what is no more than the machination of states acting in their interests; military force has a clearer metric of success or failure. But the military sees great value in examining its own history far more than does the Foreign Service, as witnessed by the extent to which the institutions study their own respective experiences. Most military officers have been schooled on General Lee's tactics at Chancellorsville or Washington's Jacobin strategy during the revolution; no diplomats have been schooled on John Adams' tactics in Holland or have made comparative studies of Adams', Franklin's, and Jefferson's tactics in Paris.

Among the detrimental effects of this lack of education on their own statecraft is a tendency to overstate both the achievements of the past and the difficulties of the present. This is especially true in the context of European diplomatic relationships, the deepest and most consequential international relations the United States has had for most of its history. Even after the cold war ended, a predominance of talented Foreign Service officers tended to be Europeanists, and they have tended to consider European relationships paramount.[8] But even in a Euro-centric Foreign Service, its specialists are generalists. Most are well informed on current European developments; virtually none would know that President Eisenhower considered the "NATO idea" to be failing in 1954.[9] As a result, they consider the past a time of comity and the present unduly complicated.

Few serious observers of the culture of the Foreign Service have been as stringent in their castigation as former Secretary of State Dean Acheson, who led the department in the post-war period so often held up as the apogee of diplomatic success. He described it this way on December 8, 1941:

> Washington awoke, a capital at war. The indecisions, hesitations, and doubts of the past year, the pretenses and fumblings, were gone. Argument over, the country and its capital turned to what Americans like and do best, action. In a few months half a continent and a hundred and thirty million people were transformed into the greatest military power the world had seen. Amid this burst of energy the State Department stood

breathless and bewildered like an old lady at a busy intersection during rush hour. All around it vigorous, effective people were purposefully on their way to do jobs that needed doing. Nowhere was this more true than in making and executing plans for economic dealings with friends, enemies, and neutrals all over the world. The object was to corner all useful materials for our side and preclude the enemy from getting them. These were not operations for which State Department officers were trained or fitted, though they reeked of foreign policy.[10]

Nor did Acheson believe the Department adapted once war had been joined:

> If the Army and Navy were unprepared for war, the State Department was no less so. It never did seem to find its place . . . my memory (perhaps an unfair or incomplete one) is of a department without direction, composed of a lot of busy people working hard and usefully but as a whole not functioning as a foreign office. It did not chart a course to be furthered by the success of our arms, or to aid or guide our arms. Rather it seems to have been adrift, carried hither and yon by the currents of war or pushed about by collisions with more purposeful craft.[11]

Acheson was even less charitable about the State Department's post-war planning, generally considered the zenith of American diplomacy because it developed the occupation of Germany and Japan and is credited for inventing the architecture of alliances and international organizations that continue even now as the infrastructure of politics among nations. Acheson considers State detached from "the practicalities of current problems and power relationships," causing it to be "absorbed in platonic planning of utopia."[12]

All of which leads to the conclusion that even at its best, at the time we look back on as Elysian for American diplomacy, its practitioners gave their performance low marks and considered the institution itself poorly equipped for what was required of it. Much was accomplished, but there wasn't a golden age of American diplomacy so much as there is a current deficiency in understanding the actual history of American diplomacy. And as Joseph Ellis has argued of the Founding Fathers, we do a disservice to those who accomplished great things to cast them in marble, for it understates what they achieved as men imperfect and fallible but persevering, and absolves us of holding ourselves to the same high standard.[13] It was never easy, diplomats were never accorded pride of place in decision-making, politics always intruded on policy, outsized personalities had outsized effects both good and bad. But how these factors affected American diplomacy and who managed them adroitly ought to be essential knowledge for our diplomats. That diplomats do not consider it so is a telling fingerprint of the Foreign Service culture.

Suspect Loyalty

The shameful behavior of Congress and so many other institutions of American government—especially the FBI—in the McCarthy era has left an enduring scar on the psyche of the Foreign Service. Senator Joseph McCarthy was recklessly destructive in his tactics, wrong in many particulars about communist influence in the State Department, and horribly damaging to many innocent individuals; but he was not entirely wrong about communist sympathies in the department and the existence of Soviet spies in its ranks.

In some ways, the spy scandals of the 1950s are the defining basis for diplomats' belief that they are neither understood nor appreciated by the American body politic. There were, after all, both communist sympathizers and Soviet spies in other institutions of our government and in our society more broadly. There is no evidence the State Department was particularly susceptible to the lure, at least not any more than Americans of comparable education and economic standing. American diplomats served courageously in dangerous postings then as now. But the State Department was particularly targeted by Senator McCarthy, and less able to defend itself because it lacked the deference shown to military members in uniform and because the nature of diplomatic work requires involvement with foreign governments and individuals. Diplomats tended to have elite educations and fewer links to organizations of American civil society, making them less sympathetic figures.

None of this justifies what diplomats were subjected to by McCarthyite investigations; but it does help explain the pervading sense in the Foreign Service that continues to some extent even to this day of being more vulnerable to criticism than other professionals involved in national security. And yet, it was an alumnus of American diplomacy, the founding director of the U.S. Information Agency, Edward R. Murrow, who did so much to publicize the unsubstantiated nature of allegations and call for Americans to uphold their values, something that gets overlooked in the narrative of the Foreign Service as uniquely vulnerable.

Lesser Among Equals

Two factors are crucial in understanding how the Department of State lost its stature as the primary means of American engagement in the world: first, the overwhelming force of arms in World War II and subsequent creation of a Department of Defense; and second, the progressive anemia the department has been subjected to by chronic underfunding and a lack of institutional leadership. The first requires little explanation; the second is a more complicated story of institutional failure.

Before 1945, the U.S. government was both simpler and smaller. As agencies and departments proliferated and undertook specialized functions, State authority over foreign policy ebbed, for example with the creation of the Office of the United States Trade Representative in 1963. Trade is an essential component of diplomacy and traditionally one of the central means by which our country exercises soft power. Yet, Congress chose to separate trade promotion and even negotiation of trade treaties from the Department of State. USTR's official history cites "Congressional interest in achieving a better balance between competing domestic and international interests in formulating and implementing U.S. trade policy," meaning that Congress had determined the Department of State insufficiently attentive to the domestic economic concerns affected by trade.[14]

In the 1970s, Congress elevated the trade representative to the cabinet, making that person the peer of the secretary of state, and designated them the "principal advisor to the President on trade policy and on the impact of other U.S. government policies on international trade." That is, Congress gave the trade representative authority to grade the work of the secretary of state and contest international policies developed by the State Department that might inhibit trade. Legislation in the 1980s put USTR in the chair for developing interagency policies, literally unseating State, and designated USTR as the implementing agency for enforcement vis-à-vis foreign countries of U.S. rights under trade agreements. This is government-speak for allowing the trade representative to determine when retaliatory tariffs or sanctions are applied, another substantial diversion of responsibility from the diplomatic arm of government.

State's failure to defend its prerogative as the substantive expert and principal interlocutor on trade was a grave blow to the capacity of the Department of State to execute its function of leading the development and conduct of American foreign policy. Yet the story repeated serially as the Foreign Service became more generalist and the department decreasingly able to persuade either the White House or the Congress to uphold its authority.

Creation of the U.S. Agency for International Development followed a very similar trajectory to USTR. In amending the Foreign Assistance Act, Congress in 1961 separated military from non-military aid, intending to increase public support for long-term development projects. From its inception, USAID was designed to free development assistance from the sullying connection to advancing American short-term political interests. USAID's official history rather unselfconsciously states that "it was thought that to renew support for foreign assistance at existing or higher levels, to address the widely-known shortcomings of the previous assistance structure, and to achieve a new mandate for assistance to developing countries, the entire program had to be 'new'."[15]

That proved unpersuasive, Congress declining to pass foreign assistance legislation beginning in 1971. Yet the Department of State not only didn't prevent establishment of development assistance independent from diplomacy, it has failed in the intervening four decades to persuade Congress to reconnect them. More than twenty federal agencies conduct foreign economic assistance programs; the secretary of state and the director of foreign assistance together have authority over fewer than half of the programs.[16]

While the secretary of state is nominally also the head of the Agency for International Development, that agency operates with such independence that a separate cabinet post is regularly advocated by development lobbyists on the argument that the secretary of state is an insufficient advocate for development. And the biggest bureaucratic winner in the 2010 Quadrennial Diplomacy and Development Review is unquestionably USAID, which has regained much of the autonomy the Bush administration had sought to curtail and place under diplomatic authority.

The closest parallel action by Congress with respect to military policy was the creation in 1985 of a combatant command dedicated to—and an assistant secretary of defense for—special operations and low-intensity conflict. Even there, Congress acted in the context of an overall reform of defense operations intended to make the department more—not less—coherent and left the responsibility in military hands. Congressional concern that the institution paid insufficient attention to a crucial component of its activity was responded to by the department with reassurance the institution would improve sufficiently to keep the activity in house (granted, the standard is higher for creating a separate military organization outside Pentagon purview). In a grace note of deference to congressional interest, the assistant secretary position has typically been filled by an appointee coming from Capitol Hill. Simply put, DOD has a much better record of working with Congress to address congressional concerns.

Part of the reason for chipping off elements of diplomacy from the purview of the Department of State has been the way State itself comprises its expertise. The Foreign Service defines itself aggressively as "generalists," leaving the "specialist" work to civil servants in the department. Yet the definition of what constitutes specialized expertise has been broadening, while the general skill set of diplomats has not kept pace with the changing international order.

The department's own Quadrennial Diplomacy and Development Review admits "we need experts in fields as diverse as public diplomacy and crisis response, public health and food security, gender issues, arms control and police training, counterradicalization and management. And we need them now."[17] But these are not specialized areas of expertise, they are core skills for America's diplomats. In what are Foreign Service officers expert if not public diplomacy, crisis response, police training, and countering radical narratives? These are—or should be—common skills given that the responsibility for conduct of the activities has long resided with the State Department.

Congress would not keep carving out constituent elements of diplomacy if it considered the State Department successful in promoting those interests and using those tools effectively. State has suffered from either diminishing capacity in the conduct of its mission or diminishing ability to persuade Congress of its effectiveness—or both.

Militarization of Foreign Policy

Formation of a unified Department of Defense after World War II and the retention of a very large military and armaments industry created an institutional competitor to the Department of State on foreign policy issues, one more influenced by military perspectives and much more prolifically funded than State has been for the intervening half century. The disparity in standing size and budget may go some way toward explaining a structural imbalance in American foreign policy (bringing to mind General Hugh Shelton urging greater non-defense spending because "if all you have is a hammer every problem is a nail"), but it cannot explain the enormous flow tide of civilian responsibilities into military channels in recent years. Nor can the obvious shock of the terrorist attacks of 9/11, as it increased funding to State as well as to Defense; capacities that had to be nurtured in the military could as justifiably have been grown in civilian agencies.

Nowhere in recent years has the atrophying of State Department authority been clearer than with respect to the Department of Defense. Some of this is the inevitable consequence of being at war: the subordination of other goals to battlefield success, the necessary sequencing of activity dictated by the security circumstances, the danger accepted by military personnel but understandably taken more cautiously by civilians. The enduring nature of conflicts in which we are now involved has made more difficult the transition of authority back into civilian hands, as has the continued danger for civilians operating in Iraq and Afghanistan.[18]

But even with those caveats, the shift of responsibility to the military of functions traditionally undertaken by diplomats has been marked. The American Academy of Diplomacy acknowledges that "our military has taken on responsibilities traditionally met by diplomats and development experts."[19] The Stimson Center, in arguing for greater spending on foreign affairs, cautions that "The "militarization of diplomacy" is noticeably expanding."[20] The most succinct and vivid description (also cited by the American Academy of Diplomacy) is from Matt Armstrong: diplomacy wears combat boots.[21]

Even where explicitly given authority, as it was in 2005 for government-wide leadership on reconstruction and development, State has not been able to provide the personnel, readiness, flexibility, agility, and funding to support and shape reconstruction and stabilization programs.[22] And even where it has been given money, State has not matched other resources to the need: military assistance funding channeled through State has increased by 54 percent but staffing by specialists in politico-military affairs has declined by more than two-thirds.[23]

Where Foreign Service officers used to advise governments, members of the military in both Iraq and Afghanistan have more often been the preferred interlocutors because they are seen by governments as more able to solve problems. Programs that have traditionally been run by the Department of State, such as police training, have become major components of military operations in both Iraq and Afghanistan. This is in part the result of the need for large commitments of people and money, neither of which the State Department has, and the ability to oversee them.

During operations in Iraq, the U.S. military has assisted the Iraqi Department of the Interior in training 410,000 police officers and has built an Iraqi military of 245,000 members.[24]

But the migration of responsibilities is not just a function of dangerous environments, magnitude of resources, or urgency of tasks. In both Iraq and Afghanistan, military leaders have been the key conduit to those countries' political leaders because the diplomats could not build the necessary relationships—the key diplomatic task. When given responsibility for essential programs, such as police training in Iraq, the State Department contracted out the work and provided weak oversight.[25]

These failures go to the department's capacity to prepare for and carry out central diplomatic functions. In the case of Iraq, the Department of State has had nearly three years since the signing of the U.S.-Iraqi security agreement to plan for the responsibilities that would migrate to it as military forces departed the country. Yet it has, by all accounts other than its own, failed to effectively do so.

Most importantly for the purposes of understanding how to improve the performance of the State Department, in those cases where diplomats were the center of gravity (such as Iraq during Ambassador Ryan Crocker's tenure) it was as the result of an individual's excellence, not the institution functioning well to prepare diplomats for their tasks and responsibilities.[26]

In an effort to build the Department of State into military operations, the military's combatant command staffs have created senior positions for diplomats.[27] Most regional military commands now have senior diplomatic "deputy commanders," although they are not authorized to act as functional deputies. They are instead senior diplomatic advisors to military commanders (a position already extant, but staffed at lower seniority as political advisors). This is a poor substitute for creating cohesive diplomatic action across regions by providing the military commander a diplomatic counterpart of similar responsibility and command of resources or by building the capacity of embassies and the department to perform their functions without military support.

The State of State

The Department of State employee roster consists of roughly 7,800 Foreign Service Officers, 11,000 civil servants, and 42,000 foreign nationals.[28] In 2009, 16,000 applicants took the written test to join the Foreign Service, competing for roughly 1,000 job offers.[29] The people selected have college degrees and eleven years of prior work experience before coming into the Foreign Service.[30] Two-thirds of the people selected for the Foreign Service come in with post-graduate degrees, and 80 percent of them have lived overseas.[31]

Foreign Service officers are awarded "tenure" after four years; 95 percent of the serving officers receive tenure. The mid-career stage of the Foreign Service can run twenty-seven years before selection into the Senior Foreign Service; one-third of Foreign Service officers make the cut into the Senior Foreign Service.[32] On average, a third of their career is spent in Washington at the State Department's headquarters. Twenty-five percent of all our diplomats are concentrated in only thirty countries; more than 2,000 are in Iraq and Afghanistan.[33] They are generalists rather than specialists, and receive almost no training across their careers except for languages.

The department's 11,000 civil servants are considered the reservoir of specialized expertise. They have no obligation to serve overseas and are not subject to "up or out" career provisions.[34] Among the many areas considered specialized and technical expertise by the State Department are environmental affairs (such as climate change, global health issues, and epidemiology);

control and nonproliferation of nuclear weapons and other weapons of mass destruction; energy; telecommunications; religious practices and human rights; refugee matters; and the law of the sea.[35] The Department of State, by its own admission, acquires rather than develops this expertise in its Foreign Service officers and civil servants.[36]

If sheer numbers were the nature of the State Department's deficiencies, the problem should by now have been corrected. Since 2003, there have been three separate initiatives—one by each of the secretaries—to increase the number of diplomats. From a baseline of 5,400 diplomats, Secretary Powell added 1,200 Foreign Service and civil service personnel through his Diplomatic Readiness Initiative. Secretary Rice added another 1,400 with her Transformational Diplomacy program, and Secretary Clinton plans another 2,300 as part of Diplomacy 3.0.[37] All three have been funded by Congress and the department has recruited the personnel. Yet, by evidence of the department's own quadrennial review and spending requests, it is nowhere nearer to having the people needed to perform its critical functions.

This connects back to the department's culture. It is assigning personnel to the functions it values rather than the functions for which the personnel were justified and funded. State's explanation for the continuing shortfall is the extraordinarily complex nature of current challenges and the impossibility of meeting those challenges with current resources. Once again, organizational culture defeats leadership intent.

The one area in which State commits resources to training is for language proficiency. Yet of the 44 percent of all overseas positions that, according to department criteria, require competence in the local language, 25 percent were vacant and more than 25 percent of the rest were filled by incumbents who lacked the necessary level of competence.[38] The Government Accountability

Office estimates the shortfall of language skills to exceed 50 percent in some critical Arabic-speaking countries.[39]

Public diplomacy has consistently been identified as essential in the war against al Qaeda and in the broader effort to reduce anti-Americanism, yet "today's staff of 1,332 Americans is 24% less than the comparable 1986 level of 1,742."[40]

The Embassy of the Future Commission considered State's personnel system one of the department's major failures.[41] The head of State's Resource Management and Analysis Division admits that, concerning the analysis of how many staff the department needs, "these numbers change on a weekly basis."[42]

In other words, the human resources department of the organization has not done a rigorous analysis of the personnel needs of the department before initiating the largest hiring in more than thirty years. That State cannot tell how many people it needs to carry out its essential functions suggests problems in addition to under-staffing.

Most egregious of the deficiencies at State is not quantity but quality. The Stimson Center (a sympathetic observer) concludes that Foreign Service officers are deficient in "foreign language fluency, advanced area knowledge, leadership and management ability, negotiating and pre-crisis conflict mediation/resolution skills, public diplomacy, foreign assistance, post-conflict/stabilization, job specific functional expertise, strategic planning, program development, implementation and evaluation, and budgeting."[43] And this occurs even though State begins with staff members who come into the service with graduate educations and, on average, eleven years of work experience. The State Department fails to foster the talent it possesses.[44]

Secretary Powell in particular sought to help develop the skills of the Foreign Service and civil service by creating a career development program; his justification for the additional personnel was to build time into their career timelines to permit professional education. The career development program sought to establish standards for advancement: development of operational effectiveness in two geographic regions, coursework to improve leadership, language proficiency, and deployments to hardship posts. Standards were grandfathered to allow gradual attainment; even so, they have not been met.[45]

Despite Secretary Powell's 1,200 additional personnel, Secretary Rice's 1,400, and Secretary Clinton's projected 2,300, the Department of State has not created the training and educational opportunities the Diplomatic Readiness Initiative was designed to provide. No time has been built into the career tracks of diplomats for the pursuit of knowledge and skills to better prepare them for the needs of the Foreign Service or the responsibilities of future assignments. With the exception of two mandatory short leadership courses, training other than in languages remains voluntary. Instead, the new hires have been diverted to fill existing staffing gaps or new needs at embassies in Iraq and Afghanistan.

The department is midway through the projected 25 percent increase in hiring as part of Diplomacy 3.0, which plans to increase the size of the Foreign Service to 8,800.[46] Because of the surge of recent hiring, more than half of the Foreign Service members have less than ten years in the department and nearly a third of the diplomatic corps has less than five years experience.[47] Both State and USAID continue to contract out large components of their institutional activity, even though a quarter of contracted work has been assessed by the Office of Personnel Management to be either inherently governmental or mission-critical.[48] This screams out for an accounting of what State actually needs to be successful: what functions, performed by how many people, and with what expertise?

Diplomacy 3.0 does not include an educational or training component, although the Stimson Center concludes "today's Foreign Service does not have to a sufficient degree the knowledge, skills,

abilities, and outlooks needed to equip career diplomats to conduct 21st-century diplomacy."[49]

What professional development does occur has traditionally
been informal mentoring provided by senior diplomats to junior
ones. It is a problematic model, depending as it does on individuals without any institutional compensation for their inadequacies
or biases in whom to invest in, and how. But even if the mentoring
model worked well, State's expanded hiring in recent years has
so increased the proportion of junior diplomats that the mentoring model cannot be sustained—the people providing the mentoring lack the experience to do so. Needs have overwhelmed the
system to such an extent that the American Academy of Diplomacy suggests bringing retired Foreign Service officers back to
serve as "roving mentors."

This is not a recipe for success.

The Market-Clearing Rate

State reports that in 2009 (the last year for which data is available), 16,000 people took the Foreign Service Exam, hoping
to be selected for the 1,000 hiring slots.[50] This is an applicant-
to-acceptance ratio worthy of one of the country's very best
universities.[51]

Supply is dramatically outstripping demand; in a free market, this means compensation could be reduced until the excess
of qualified applicants were priced out of the equation. To put it
bluntly: we are over-paying our diplomats. The market clearing
rate—the pay rate at which supply and demand would come into
alignment—is significantly less than what we are offering in compensation. By definition, there are more applicants than positions,
so downward price pressure would drive some applicants to other
professions.

The contrast to military practice is again illustrative. The military services expend considerable institutional effort in determining the skills that make someone suitable as a Soldier, Sailor, Airman, or Marine. They advertise and recruit for the skills they want, varying compensation such as combat pay and reenlistment bonuses to ensure adequate representation of specific skills. They analyze who leaves the force and why, then develop targeted programs for retention (educational benefits at the eight-year point, retirement benefits at twenty years on active duty). They shed or retrain personnel with skills no longer necessary (artillery) or no longer a priority when resources get tight (an example is the Army eliminating foreign area officers in the force reductions of the 1990s). The Department of State does none of these things.[52]

At the very least, the magnitude of demand suggests the Department of State has the luxury of setting exacting standards for the Foreign Service. But are the people who apply for the Foreign Service the people we want as our diplomats? State rightly touts the achievements of those selected. The Department also, not surprisingly, believes the examination process requires applicants to demonstrate proficiency in skills necessary for success as diplomats.

Yet State's own evaluation in the Quadrennial Diplomacy and Development Review makes clear that the hiring process does not produce what is needed. It "highlights some specific new skills and knowledge sets State needs to address the challenges of our increasingly complex world: familiarity with new technology; scientific training; security sector and rule of law experience; expertise in humanitarian assistance, gender issues, energy security, environmental issues, and macroeconomics."[53]

The State Department's willingness to hire people skilled at the new demands of American diplomacy—and even its institutional acknowledgement of the new demands—are called into question by the Stimson Center, a think tank that counts itself among State's strongest defenders. One of the central criticisms of Stimson's *Foreign Affairs Budget for the Future* is that "the mechanics of the personnel system must provide individuals with the skills and incentives to carry out the expanded functions and purposes of all of the categories examined, and the culture of the Department of State must accept those new or expanded functions as legitimate and important."[54]

State personnel managers will surely worry that reducing pay will reduce quality. This is a legitimate concern, but it's one experienced by all organizations and can be controlled for by State itself in setting standards. State develops the examination and interview process that screens applicants; if applicants pass those hurdles, they are qualified. By not compromising its hiring standards and by raising compensation if too few qualified applicants are presented, State can protect itself.

Part of the reason we over-pay our diplomats is that the market for their services is most decidedly not free. It is rigidified by a powerful Foreign Service Union, a corporate board (the Congress) that exercises its fiduciary responsibilities predominantly by corporate social responsibility initiatives rather than shareholder value, and no market feedback of the kind provided by stock prices to publicly traded corporations.

There are many possible reasons so many Americans are seeking to become diplomats. They include a surfeit of patriotism enduring from the 9/11 attacks on the World Trade Center and the Pentagon; the desire to serve their country in time of war; excitement at the possibilities associated with "operating at the edges" as our diplomacy evolves away from capitols, including our own; the satisfaction of making a difference on problems of enormous magnitude; the unusually high rate of white-collar unemployment associated with the 2008 financial crisis; and surely many other motivations.

We don't actually know applicants' motivations, because the Department of State does not survey their attitudes. There is no market research of the kind that assists military recruiting efforts. State hires so infrequently, and has such a glut of applicants when it does, that it surveys only the composition of its hires (race, gender, education, years of work experience), not their motivations. And because the Foreign Service Exam is extolled by the Foreign Service personnel system as producing the diplomats adept at the skills valued by the Foreign Service, there has been no pressure to rethink—beyond race and gender to substantive qualifications— whether the applicants coming into the system have the skill sets, including motivations, to be the diplomatic representatives our nation needs.

As with most policies of the State Department, language is the exception: State has recently begun to target applicants with language skills in prized areas, especially Mandarin Chinese and Arabic.[55] Native speakers of those languages are now fast-tracked through the hiring process, provided they agree to serve two tours of duty in postings utilizing those languages. But beyond languages, there is no effort to identify applicants with entrepreneurial experience, information technology proficiency, prior military service, or other qualifications that might foreshadow a greater resiliency for the Foreign Service at the challenges it has identified as needing strengthened personnel competence.

Not only are these attributes not tracked and advertised for in initial diplomatic hires, they are not compensated for by mid-career hires. An undersecretary for management once explained the absence of mid-career recruitment on the basis that no matter how skilled people from outside the Foreign Service might be, they didn't have the knowledge to work successfully in the Foreign Service. By this argument, the information management executive from Google would have nothing to contribute to American diplomacy because she had not apprenticed through the system. The Foreign Service is content to replicate itself rather than evolve, and has been permitted to.

In seeking to open its personnel system to greater diversity, State has recently declared itself in support of hiring of specialized talent . . . from its own civil service. That is, State will seek to broaden its expertise by converting the category of service (from civil to foreign) for personnel already within its ranks. It believes by doing so it can provide better opportunities for people who have a demonstrated ability to adapt to the culture of the Foreign Service.[56]

Needless to say, this does not expand the expertise of the department. It also perpetuates the bias that bolstering the existing culture of the Foreign Service is an inherent good, something to be optimized as personnel decisions are considered.

Mid-career hires from outside the system tend not to stay in the Foreign Service, according to the undersecretary for management, because they do not meld into the Foreign Service way of doing business. What this conveys is that State does not have a culture malleable enough to benefit from the diversity outsiders bring into the system; it expects them to conform, rather than for the system to adapt to utilize their differences.

Military experience with racial and gender integration suggests that below the level of about 10 percent, introduction of difference tends toward alienation of both the majority and the minority; beyond 10 percent, not only does the minority adapt to the majority, but it also changes the majority culture. Applied to the need for greater experiential diversity in the Foreign Service, several possible alternatives to its approach could be explored: increasing the number of mid-career hires, clustering them in locations where they can provide each other support, giving them dedicated mentors to help them understand the institutional culture in which they are operating, providing them levers to effect change in the organization.

The Department of State's need is not for more diplomats who can conform to existing institutional culture, it is for a burgeoning of diversity in skills that can transform State's institutional culture to be more entrepreneurial, more tech-savvy, more activist than descriptive, and with a different balance of risk-tolerance inherent in how it does its job. Needless to say, such a frame of reference would need to be encouraged, and possibly imposed, on the Department of State's personnel system.

Deeply engrained in the personnel system's approach is the assumption that it is hiring people for the length of their working lives. Barriers to entry are high (infrequent hiring), selection for advancement is nearly guaranteed (95 percent of officers entering the Foreign Service become tenured), and lateral entry is discouraged and also lacks support structures to facilitate success. The Foreign Service has only a 4 percent attrition rate, well below all other government agencies.[57]

Yet why should it be that a bias for long-term service drives the personnel system? With a 16:1 applicant ratio, State could afford to hire diplomats in numbers and with skills specialized to short-term needs; it does not require longevity to ensure its ranks are filled.

Fully half the ambassadors at U.S. missions are political appointees. They are not concentrated in vacation paradises but are in charge of embassies in some of America's most important and closely allied countries, such as the United Kingdom and China, and the multilateral institutions of the United Nations, NATO, and the European Union. They are selected because of their commitment to the current president's program, not their ability to conform to the standards of the Foreign Service. And overwhelmingly, politically appointed diplomats view the career Foreign Service as impediments to the president's agenda, not allies in its advancement.

This could be explained as a burden diplomacy bears by presidential prerogative, except that the State Department itself conveys the same message by requiring no additional education for its professionals as their responsibilities enlarge nor training beyond that acquired on the job. The current director of State's Office of the Coordinator for Reconstruction and Stabilization, a genuinely outstanding twenty-seven-year veteran of the Foreign Service and career ambassador, received no training at all other than language.[58]

If the standard of performance were evidently disparate between career ambassadors and political appointees, it would make the case for tenured Foreign Service. If percolating up through the system made diplomats appreciatively better than those who parachute in on political appointments, State would have a stronger argument for its system of producing senior diplomats. But the data are not conclusive; individuals perform well and poorly on both sides of the ledger, suggesting individual attributes matter much more than institutional preparation.

Moreover, the career ambitions of people entering the Foreign Service are not commensurate with the "lifer" assumptions of the personnel managers. Studies by futurists extrapolating trends out into the longer term suggest that students concluding their graduate education now are likely to have as many as six different careers—not jobs, careers—in the course of their professional lives. The rate of change in technology, decline of behemoth corporations that undertook to provide social benefits like medical coverage, restlessness of talent, and opportunities created by reduced international barriers all suggest the people coming into the Foreign Service may want less job security than the profession is offering. At the very least it suggests that the professional peers of those coming into the Foreign Service have those wants, and if incoming Foreign Service officers want more stability, we ought to give considerable thought to whether we are encouraging something at odds with the needs of American diplomacy.

How Much Is Enough?

In assessing its personnel needs, the State Department uses vacancy rates. That is, it determines how many people are required by counting desks, but their staffing models do not incorporate an assessment of whether those desks need to be filled.[59] For example, State's narrative of the decimation of diplomatic power with the end of the cold war highlights that it opened twenty new embassies in former Soviet republics without any additional staff. At first blush that sounds impressive, except that it pockets the reduction in workload associated with the end of the Soviet Union and the end of cold war tensions in both Eastern and Western Europe. The embassy in East Germany went away completely, as did requirements for working with dissident movements and monitoring Soviet military presence. But these positive reductions in diplomatic activity are not factored into State's explanation. Theirs is a calculus of only counting increased demand.

In fact, we have no means of assessing whether cascading personnel from existing European embassies to create new ones should have entailed additional personnel, because the Department of State does not measure how busy its personnel are. How much work is being accomplished is not weighed in determining personnel requirements; State does not consider that relevant information. Instead, State "models its overseas staffing configuration on the basis of policy conditions and working environments rather than quantifiable workload."

Without a metric that equalizes workload, State is left free to devalue consular activity, where the workload is generally highest, while concentrating resources in other areas, such as engaging with multilateral institutions (e.g., the United Nations). In the latter, "engagement in the process" is used as the criterion for success, rather than actual outcomes achieved.

State's internal assessment of personnel needs is weighted wholly to subjective factors that further reinforce the value of work the institutional culture already values. Advocates for continuing to increase the number of diplomats complain that post-9/11 increases have been predominantly in consular and diplomatic security rather than new staff for multilateral organizations, international law, economics, science and technology, public/private partnerships, and international organizations.[60] By that, they mean that the terrorist attacks on the United States should have resulted in more involvement in activities they are already optimized to, rather than increasing security for embassies and screening people applying for visas, even though those are critical vulnerabilities highlighted by attacks on American embassies in the past fifteen years.

An important measure of institutional transformation is what no longer needs doing, or no longer needs doing in the ways it has previously been done. State's model for determining personnel requirements has not incorporated a subtraction function; it is all addition. Improvements in technology that make workers more efficient have not been folded into State calculations of "vacancies." Improvements in communications and availability of information have not been incorporated into State's evaluation of the frequency and type of reporting to which diplomatic posts allocate their time. Metrics have not been developed enabling comparison of different diplomatic functions and their relative success in different environments.

State has not even undertaken a serious review of what functions need to be performed in embassies overseas and which can be considered back-office support and relocated to more secure or cost-effective locations. The Embassy of the Future project recommended back-office support be regionalized or repatriated to the United States.⁶¹ Such a move would not only increase security, it would give State a stronger domestic constituency. American military forces dramatically shifted their global posture in the past twenty years as technology allowed functions like weather forecasting and drone piloting to be undertaken remotely.

Why is it that back-office functions need to be performed by Foreign Service and civil service personnel or by non-Americans overseas, rather than outsourcing payroll and administrative functions domestically? State's Quadrennial Diplomacy and Development Review proposes giving foreign nationals much greater opportunity for careers and advancement within our diplomatic service; it ought at least to assess the alternative of reducing our footprint overseas to those activities that require foreign presence and engagement.

The number of American diplomats has increased by 50 percent since 2001 without a rigorous assessment of how many people are needed, performing what functions in what locations around the world. Before further increases to staffing are supported, we should challenge State to develop analytic means of justifying current staffing levels.

Deficient Education

The State Department treats education as a prerequisite for hiring, not a continuing requirement to prepare personnel for subsequent responsibilities. It is as if Major League Baseball pitchers only threw in games, never in practice sessions with careful coaching by experts to refine their delivery, correct creeping bad habits, and expand their repertoire of pitches. When diplomats come in the door, they are treated as though they have all the knowledge and skill necessary for the profession. The only instruction provided is mentoring by senior diplomats, the equivalent of veteran pitchers coaching rookies.

Continuing education is available—on diplomats' own time and by their own initiative. It may be marginally helpful in consideration by promotion boards and for assignment selection, but the overriding attitude is that Foreign Service and civil service employees who can be made available for educational opportunities are expendable. State's most talented up-and-coming staff do not avail themselves of educational opportunities; diverging from the work at hand is considered bad form.

The State Department has no cohesive program that identifies the skills which diplomats will need as their responsibilities burgeon at higher levels in the profession. There is no body of knowledge which experts in the profession have determined essential to understanding and performing well. There is no set of skills on which diplomats are tested to determine proficiency. There is no body of case studies developed to compare different approaches to similar problems. There is no doctrine developed to guide activity in key areas of performance. In short, we are not setting our diplomats up to be successful.

By taking this approach to education, the department is conveying to its personnel and beyond that it does not respect its own people enough to invest in them and that it does not respect the practice of diplomacy enough to believe those engaged in it need to develop skills to be successful at it. State may complain that Congress does not respect the professionalism of the Foreign Service in the way it respects the military, but it is folly to expect outsiders to have an appreciation the institution does not accord itself.

State representatives would reply that it continuously engages in educating diplomats through mentoring. They describe State's model as apprenticeship in the manner of professional guilds. Such a model is fundamentally unfair, however, as it stakes junior diplomats' prospects to the abilities and willingness of senior mentors to invest in their development. Senior personnel are not trained or evaluated on their contributions as mentors; it is an additional duty, not a line responsibility. Moreover, this approach personalizes what should be a level playing field in which the institution invests equally in the prospects of its professionals.

But the most damning criticism of State's education model comes from its own graduates. The American Academy of Diplomacy (an advocacy group founded by retired diplomats that undertakes studies of the profession) concludes that the model is failing America's diplomats: "formal training has grown in importance, as traditional means of learning the skills of the diplomatic profession—on-the-job training and guidance from more senior officers—have lost much of their effectiveness."[62] The model has crumpled under the pressure of so many junior hires in the past decade creating more demand for mentoring than senior staff can provide.

The AAD's proposal is modest: a roving band of retired Foreign Service officers who circuit-ride embassies to provide mentoring. While well-intentioned and conscientiously designed for affordability, this correction is wholly inadequate. It demonstrates just how badly State is in need of a systematic approach to education.

Contrasts with Military Culture

The comparisons between diplomatic and military culture give some insight into why the State Department has a more difficult time both winning support and making the best of its many assets. While both the military and diplomacy are forms of national service, the culture of service is much more fundamental to the ethos of the American military than it is to our diplomats. Our service men and women take an oath to defend the Constitution and the system inculcates subordination to the civilian leadership as a core value of its professionalism.

Even on an issue where the military feels both misunderstood and unappreciated, such as homosexuals serving openly in its ranks, the military from leadership to new inductee understand that their only acceptable action is to salute smartly and carry out the will of the civilian leadership if they want to remain in the service. Thus we see General James Amos, the Commandant of the Marine Corps, who in December 2010 warned that changing the policy could cost lives, being praised in January 2011 by gay rights groups for implementing the policy.[63]

The Foreign Service culture has a different ethos, one much less responsive to the policy choices of the country's political leadership. It was most visible during the Iraq war, when diplomats spoke openly of their hostility to the president proceeding without a United Nations Security Council mandate and when the department had difficulty filling posts in Iraq. But diplomats' opinion that they are protecting America from the poor choices of its elected leadership is not specific to Iraq; it is much more widespread and long-standing. It is not uncommon for Foreign Service officers to avoid defending policies with which they do not agree. Dean Acheson observed in his memoirs that "the attitude that presidents and secretaries may come and go but the Department goes on forever has led many presidents to distrust and dislike the Department of State."[64]

In addition to the deep ethos of service, military culture has a unity of purpose seldom found in civilian culture. The military's job is to fight and win the nation's wars. The Marine Corps takes this focus even further, instilling the idea that every Marine is a rifleman with all other military specialties supporting. While such focus conceals a diversity of functions underpinning the successful conduct of that purpose, it is revealing that the Department of

State's description of its mission struggles to convey simply the purpose of the organization.

The State Department describes the essential functions of diplomacy to be:

★ Promoting and supporting U.S. foreign policies to foreign governments and international organizations

★ Supporting U.S. economic and commercial interests

★ Negotiating treaties and agreements to protect America's interests

★ Playing an active role in conflict prevention and crisis management

★ Informing U.S. foreign policy decision-making through reporting, analysis, and policy recommendations on political, economic, social, and other developments around the world

★ Protecting American citizens traveling abroad

★ Engaging foreign publics across the spectrum of society through active educational exchange and other public diplomacy activities

★ Supporting counternarcotics, counterterrorism, border security/law enforcement, and embassy transportation missions.[65]

The Embassy of the Future Commission prescribed a useful standard: "the truest test of the value to our nation of the U.S. diplomatic presence abroad is whether the people we ask to represent us effectively promote American values and interests."[66] There it is: promoting American values and interests effectively. It's such a simple statement; why does the State Department have such a difficult time making it? And that is the case even before folding in the purpose of USAID, which must always announce itself as not working to the same purpose as American diplomacy.

In addition to its deep commitment to service and singular sense of purpose, military culture seeks to invert the primacy of individual achievement. Warfare is a team sport. An individual is not considered successful unless everyone around them is successful, which means that military leaders are fundamentally teachers. It's a culture built to make a lot out of very little: the military takes young people with generally only a high school education, gives them the self-discipline, self-respect and skills to make them contributors while in the service, and puts them on a conveyer belt into the middle class when they leave the military. It's an extraordinary contribution to American society. The institution invests in them, identifying practices to help them succeed at future needs and both educating and training them for the responsibilities to come. It studies intensively what has worked in the past and how differences between the present and future might require different approaches. It develops doctrine to provide a starting point for learning. It provides extensive education at many different points across a career.

An Army officer, for example, would begin service with an officer's training course of six months, followed by a branch course of nearly five months to provide an initial apprenticeship in a military specialty (such as armor or artillery); another two months of leadership training or a specialized course on an element for which he or she will be responsible (such as Ranger school or a course on mechanics); then an advanced or career course for six months to prepare the soldier for company command. At a minimum, that young officer would spend a year and a half of the first decade in the Army in school. Graduate school and training with industry would add another year in that first decade, although many soldiers pursue their graduate work in conjunction with other assignments.

Intermediate level school has soldiers and their families deployed for ten months, typically all together at Fort Leavenworth, where the institution's future leaders get to know each other as majors. The common curriculum includes understanding joint, inter-agency, and multinational operations; solving complex problems systematically and under pressure; applying the perspectives of military history; the principles and values of military leadership; understanding the role of the military in a free society; and effec-tive written, oral, and electronic communication.[67]

If selected for command, the soldier would take a three-week course with other commanders. Post-command war college adds another year of schooling for soldiers remaining competitive for promotion and future command. Those selected for general officer rank fold in a three-week capstone program and specialized courses (for example, on legal requirements for courts martial). Selection for educational opportunities is seen as an indicator of continued advancement, and completion of education is required for con-sideration of future promotions. Across the course of a twenty-five-year career, that Army officer would spend at least a full four years in classrooms.

The State Department makes no such investment in its tal-ented people. Whereas the military makes a lot out of very little, in terms of the human capital coming into the system, the State Department makes a little out of a lot. Until Secretary Powell mandated leadership training, literally nothing except the intro-ductory course that all new Foreign Service officers undergo and language training were required. At the end of a twenty-five-year career, with the exception of language training, the department will have invested no more in the people who serve it than those people had coming into the institution. To the extent a Foreign Service officer grows in professional skill, it is solely the result of individual initiative and mentoring by interested superiors. That mentoring is not a formal requirement, nor are senior Foreign Service officers evaluated on the mentoring they provide.

Because the military has a learning culture, it is able to adapt more quickly to failure. Battles are followed by after-action reviews in which participants are pressed to explain their actions, determine what other choices were available to them, and consider how making different choices might have led to different consequences. Information is gathered for units and operations concurrent with the operations themselves. Historians are embedded in units and organizations to provide information for evaluation. Lessons learned are an integral part of the activity of any American military organization; they evaluate what they have done and what should be done differently, and the people doing the activity are fully involved in the evaluation as active participants. State literally does not undertake to learn from its activity; as a result, "too often officers are working without the benefit of understanding where others have succeeded."[68]

Where the military has a culture of subjugation to the institution's needs, the Foreign Service has had a culture of individual initiative where personnel assignments are concerned. It is only recently, for example, that the director general of the Foreign Service and the central personnel system have begun to refuse assignment preferences until priority posts are filled. Prior to that, the individual's choices principally determined what jobs in Washington and in embassies around the world were filled.[69]

As the result of State's inability to staff embassies during the wars in Iraq and Afghanistan, the director general has asserted the institution's prerogatives. But even there, the Foreign Service's union objected to inclusion of wartime service in evaluating diplomats for promotion. The union argued that many overseas postings are hazardous and diplomats operating in Iraq should not be compensated differently than those in other dangerous places. The argument would be more persuasive if the union had not categorized 50 percent of all overseas postings as dangerous.[70] It is simply not credible to argue that half the world is as dangerous as was Iraq, nor does such an argument build confidence in the department's judgment on other issues.

Warfare isn't an efficient undertaking. The military gets very uncomfortable when political leaders try to pare resources; it always wants a wide margin for error. This is in part because the military has a rich appreciation for how much often goes wrong in warfare, but also because resources are a proxy for commitment. Since the purpose of warfare is to compel an enemy not to continue resisting, overwhelming resourcing sends the signal of desire to win. Military leaders were intensely uncomfortable with Secretary of Defense Donald Rumsfeld shaving forces off of the plan for invading and occupying Iraq. When President George H.W. Bush expanded the 1991 Iraq War aims from defending Saudi Arabia to ejecting the Iraqi military from Kuwait, the combatant commander determined the change would require an additional hundred thousand troops; Chairman of the Joint Chiefs of Staff General Powell doubled the figure to 200,000 to provide a wider margin of error.

By contrast, the State Department identifies very modest resourcing needs. Reading the panoply of reports advocating increased foreign affairs spending, one is struck at how pathetically little the State Department and its advocates believe is needed to dramatically improve State's performance. These reports suggest that State's training deficiency could be redressed by "roving mentors" of recently retired Foreign Service officers, that all staffing gaps could be filled by a few thousand additional diplomats, and that an additional $2 billion in program funding would allow it to meet all needs.[71] This is surely the result of decades of underfunding of its activities to the point that it hesitates to ask for more when it is implausible that the difference between dire and perfect would be a few thousand people.

But this situation also shows how programmatic ignorance and chronic under-resourcing have corroded the culture of the

State Department. It no longer has big dreams and plans for making the institution flourish. When asked in 2008 to design a Diplomatic University that would be a State Department peer of the military's National Defense University, the Foreign Service Institute couldn't even imagine what it might be like or how to transform its training institute into a much more ambitious undertaking.

The resourcing issue reflects another major distinction between military and diplomatic cultures in the United States: the ability to work with Congress. State Department officials regularly complain there is "no constituency" for diplomacy and foreign assistance. They look with envy at the way members of Congress are solicitous of the concerns of military leaders and assiduous to keep military bases in their districts. Yet they act as though that outcome is a natural fact rather than the result of a consistent and long-term program of outreach to members of Congress and mobilizing interests to which Congress is responsible, like defense industries and veterans' groups. Certainly the military has advantages of scale, both in spending and personnel. But State has not designed its infrastructure to connect its activity with congressional interests.

Nor does the secretary of state involve Congress much in oversight of the department. The secretary of defense meets weekly with the congressional leadership of both the authorizing and appropriating committees to discuss issues of concern to them and also activity in the department. As a result, congressional leaders are much more likely than are their foreign affairs counterparts to give the secretary of defense latitude to reprogram funds and to give him the benefit of the doubt on both budget and policy issues.

The way State engages in budget debates creates the impression of the institution as a grievance culture, in contrast to the military's can-do institutional stamp. Take, for example, this official description:

> The United States reduced spending on diplomacy when the Cold War ended. In the 1990s, the Foreign Service in the State Department shrank as hiring was held below attrition. USAID experienced losses from attrition and layoffs—a 10% reduction in force—as well. But in the same period, the United States opened twenty-three new embassies in the states that emerged from the breakup of the Soviet Union and Yugoslavia, with no new resources provided. The resulting austerity was felt worldwide, and America's ability to conduct diplomacy deteriorated.[72]

The Pentagon would have explained all it achieved despite the spending constraints, made Congress a partner in deciding on the parameters for new embassies and activities, trumpeted its ability to realign its spending to new developments and needs, and highlighted its cost-efficiency for the American taxpayer. State comes across as resentful about the restriction, and threatens its own incompetence as the result of congressional choices. But the Department of Defense took even larger cost and personnel reductions in the same time frame without damaging its ability to protect the nation and without decrying the peace dividend. The Pentagon got ahead of the debate about reducing spending at the end of the cold war, developing a Base Force to establish a floor for spending cuts and argue for the resources it needed with analytic rigor and transparency as Congress determined spending levels.

Unstated in State's budget narrative is that the largest impediment to its funding is not the Congress, but the White House. State Department officials cannot convince Congress of the need for more money because they cannot convince the president, the Office of Management and Budget, or even their own secretary of the

need for more money; the Congress generally gives State the operating budget that the president requests. Yet State's descriptions of
its performance blame Congress in ways that make future goodwill
even less likely. Here is State's description of the dramatic effect of
Congress not funding staff positions in the newly established Office
of the Coordinator for Reconstruction and Stabilization:

> Despite the mandate of NSPD-44 (which gave State the
> interagency lead on crisis management and stabilization), from
> 2005 to 2008 funding for State did not permit hiring above
> attrition, except for security and fee-funded consular positions.
> As a consequence, posts around the world were stripped of
> personnel needed to staff the most critical jobs. By late 2008,
> 17% of Foreign Service Officer positions in high-hardship posts,
> excluding Iraq, were vacant, and 34% of mid-level positions
> were filled by officers one or two grades below the position
> grade.[73]

The office in question consisted of a few dozen staff, did not
consider its mission to encompass Iraq and Afghanistan (it was
planning for the long-term future), and was still being contested
by partisans who believed the office should be bureaucrati-
cally part of USAID. State could have easily staffed the office
from internal resources; it chose not to. State never threatened
Congress with a presidential veto over funding constraints, and
the president never spoke to the issue.

It is simply not true that between 2005 and 2008 "posts around
the world were stripped of personnel needed to staff the most critical jobs." The department had just received an additional thousand diplomats for the purpose of improving training but diverted
those thousand people to fill regular staffing needs; staffing did
increase significantly in the consular service and diplomatic
security. State did not prioritize its resources to ensure the most
important jobs were getting done—instead, it blames its managerial inadequacies on lack of resources. The inability of State to

deliver congressional support for its priorities is not an act of God; it is the result of too little positive effort.

The Pentagon would have figured out who in Congress was susceptible to persuasion on the importance of the issue and worked with them to craft a policy that could get congressional support. It would have taken journalists and members of Congress with the secretary of defense to visit field operations that would benefit from the work; named the office for a heroic diplomat who'd served doing this kind of work and was a constituent of a skeptical lawmaker; held a ceremony at which the member of Congress dedicated the office; put the training center for reconstruction and stabilization operations in the district of another key member of Congress; developed a contingency plan to fund the activity without additional money; requested the secretary to ask for authority to reprogram people and money within the department budget if Congress would not vote new money; persuaded the president to threaten to veto the appropriations bill if funding for the activity were not included; and put the secretary on all the news programs to explain the dire consequences to the country if Congress did not act responsibly. DOD gets money from Congress because it has figured out how to be persuasive to Congress; State has not.

Coming Debacle

The 2003 Iraq War exemplified the differences in institutional culture between the military and the Department of State; it is also providing a testing ground for State's ability to reclaim the responsibilities for reconstruction and stabilization assigned to it in National Security Presidential Directive 44. The Bush administration's November 2008 Strategic Framework Agreement committed the United States to withdraw all U.S. military forces from Iraq by the end of December 2011.

The drawdown of U.S. forces from a peak of 170,000 troops was intended to dramatically demonstrate to the government and people of Iraq that the United States had no ambitions for long-term control of the country. The American diplomatic and military leadership in Iraq believed well into the Obama administration that the Strategic Framework Agreement would be revised to provide a basis for continuing U.S. force presence.[74] Neither the Obama administration nor the Maliki government in Iraq exercised that option, however, requiring a transition to a solely civilian mission by 2012.

The Obama administration enthusiastically endorsed that outcome, even accelerating the timeline to end combat operations in August of 2010. Candidate Obama had campaigned on Iraq being "the wrong war," a diversion from Afghanistan, and a waste of American lives and money. Having sent a clear signal to Iraqis that the exit was the strategy, American influence declined sharply. U.S. diplomacy was ineffective in preventing Prime Minister Maliki from unconstitutionally striking hundreds of candidates from the parliamentary elections or forming a government although his party had not received the majority. We did not object either when Maliki invited the virulently anti-American Sadrist faction to join his government, precluding renegotiation of the Strategic Framework.

Even then, the Iraqi government was concerned enough about its own security to renegotiate the agreement and to provide assurances about immunity from Iraqi law for U.S. troops (a standard demand in all such U.S. status of forces agreements). The Obama administration refused the Maliki government assurances, insisting instead on approval from the Iraqi parliament. In doing so, it succeeded in raising the bar high enough that there would be no renegotiation of the agreement to allow U.S. military forces to remain in Iraq past 2011.

Despite all these signals of indifference to Iraq's fate and American influence in the country, State has chosen to make the civilian mission in Iraq a behemoth example of what "leading through civilian power" can be. There will be no residual military force for the protection of U.S. diplomats and development workers; the only military personnel will be 200 or so working from the Embassy in a military liaison mission (a job that typically involves negotiating weapons contracts, observing military exercises, and communicating with headquarters staffs).

Anthony Cordesman of the Center for Strategic and International Studies well describes the challenge of transition: ". . . it is making the transition to a civilian lead that is backed by an adequate US mix of civil aid in governance and development. It is creating a military training mission that will help Iraq become truly independent—not only of US forces but in dealing with the ambitions of all its neighbors."[75]

The plan arrived at by the military command in Iraq and the embassy, called the Joint Campaign Plan 2010, "details the transition of enduring functions, once military-led, to civilian entities including the U.S. Embassy, other international and nongovernmental organizations, as well as the government of Iraq."[76]

The State Department's plans have changed significantly since the JCP was issued, increasing the projected staff and spending requirements with each iteration. Current plans anticipate 17,000 civilian personnel in fifteen locations around Iraq, costing $25–30 billion over five years.[77] The cost of providing for diplomatic and consular functions is projected by State to rise from $120 million per month currently to $395 million per month.[78] Most civilian personnel in State's plan are projected to be non-Americans ("third country nationals" in State parlance) providing security and support under contract to the State Department. Of the 17,000 personnel, only 650 will be American diplomats.[79]

Provincial Reconstruction Teams, the integrated civil-military operations that have been successful in Iraq, will be reduced from sixteen to four. According to the Senate Foreign Relations Committee assessment, ". . . the successor sites will have reduced functional staffs, smaller operational radii, and no funding for discretionary projects."[80] So they will be not only fewer in number, but functionally much less capable.

The Commission on Wartime Contracting has identified fourteen military functions that the State Department lacks the ability to conduct:

★ Recovering killed and wounded personnel

★ Recovering damaged vehicles

★ Recovering downed aircraft

★ Clearing travel routes

★ Operations center monitoring of private security contractors

★ Private security contractor inspection and accountability services

★ Convoy security

★ Explosive-ordnance disposal

★ Counter-rocket, artillery and mortar notification

★ Counter-battery neutralization response

★ Communications support

★ Tactical operations center dispatch of armed response teams

★ Policing Baghdad's international zone

★ Maintaining electronic counter-measures, threat intelligence, and technology capabilities.[81]

State plans to have these functions performed by civilian security contractors. That this portends disaster should go without saying. The difficulties associated with secure movement also suggest the likelihood that diplomats serving outside the main embassy compound in Baghdad will be confined to their consulates or branch offices. As the Senate Foreign Relations Committee report concludes, ". . . the satellites will only be as effective as their inhabitants' ability to get off their compounds."[82]

The U.S. military has been crucial in defusing tensions between the central Iraqi government and the Kurdish regional government, establishing Combined Security Mechanisms of joint patrolling in Salah ad-Din, Kirkuk, and Diyala. The State Department has no plan for how to continue building cooperative security habits. In fact, Cordesman concludes that ". . . the State Department is strong on bluster, but remarkably silent on clear plans for action."[83] We may succeed without the plan; we will not succeed because of the plan.

In addition to the questionable soundness of the plan itself, State has not advanced its execution sufficiently to believe the civilian effort can be operational in time for the hand-over from military to civilian authority. Land use agreements have not yet been signed for the fifteen sites of U.S. outposts and transport hubs. The size and scope of the Office of Security Cooperation have not been determined. Security personnel have not been vetted or hired. The State Department's undersecretary for management has conceded that "we will continue to have a critical need for logistical and life support of a magnitude and scale of complexity that is unprecedented in the history of the Department of State. [State] does not have within its Foreign Service cadre sufficient experience and expertise to perform necessary contract oversight."[84]

Undaunted by its own internal management's concerns, the State Department glowingly describes its own performance: ". . . in Iraq, we are in the midst of the largest military-to-civilian transition since the Marshall Plan. Our civilian presence is prepared to take the lead, secure the military's gains, and build the institutions necessary for long-term stability."[85]

Major General Robert Caslen, who commanded forces in northern Iraq, has been deeply critical of the State Department's approach, saying:

> They are not actually doing the research to say this is what we need and if you don't give me this, this is what we are going to have to take away and here is the effect it will have on the effort. Rather they are going through things and saying this is what we think the piece of the pie is we're going to get and here is some stuff we could do for that money. That's all fine and good, but if you don't actually accomplish the mission in the end, then you actually fail. What good is that?[86]

The Senate Foreign Relations Committee also has serious reservations, saying that "fundamental questions remain unanswered," including whether the scope of the mission in Iraq is compatible with the resources available, including State Department capacity.[87] The committee questions whether the State Department can sustain its proposed presence without military support and the cost-effectiveness of consulates requiring 1,400 security and support personnel for only 120 diplomats.[88]

If a complete withdrawal of U.S. troops (excepting staffers in the Embassy's Office of Military Cooperation) remains U.S. and Iraqi government policy, the Senate Foreign Relations Committee report recommends that "given the prohibitive costs of security and the capacity limitations of the State Department, the United States should consider a less ambitious diplomatic presence in Iraq."[89] The Government Accountability Office is also less enthusiastic about State's ability to plan for and carry out activity.[90]

The State Department argues that its plan produces enormous savings—$65 billion over the current cost of operations in Iraq.[91]

And that is certainly true. But also inescapable is that we will be getting an awful lot less value than has been gotten from 50,000 U.S. troops in Iraq and their achievements. Moreover, an inexpensive failure is not a bargain. The $5 billion cost of civilian-led operations in Iraq will be the single largest item in the State Department's budget and twice the size of current spending for Iraq. Every single organization that has looked at the transition to "leading through civilian power" in Iraq has deep reservations about the ability of the State Department to plan for and carry out operations there.

The State Department is not solely responsible for the shortcomings of the Joint Campaign Plan for Iraq. They occur in the broader context of a presidential administration that has largely written off the war in Iraq, uninterested in it being news, bad or good, and unwilling to take assertive action beyond emphasizing a "responsible withdrawal." That a Democratic Congress twice in 2010 cut funding from the requests of a Democratic president while, overall, funding a dramatic increase in federal spending is an illustration of how little the Obama administration has invested itself in the issue.

Yet State has from the start not undertaken a capabilities-based assessment of needs for our civilian mission in Iraq, nor has it honestly assessed the limits of its ability to perform necessary tasks and explored alternatives to the current costly path of questionable utility. Instead of asserting it is ready, State should acknowledge that the demands of a civilian mission in Iraq under current circumstances are beyond its abilities. Instead of proceeding, it should reconsider alternatives: scaling down our mission in Iraq to what can be realistically achieved, revisiting the Security Agreement to permit military forces for the purpose of protecting and transporting civilian members of the mission, or partnering with Iraqi security forces to provide the necessary security.

A debacle of the kind State has set itself up for in Iraq will not just compromise American interests in Iraq, it will discredit the important effort to strengthen our non-military institutions. As the American Academy of Diplomacy concludes, ". . . the massive U.S. engagement in Iraq and Afghanistan has called into question both NSPD-44 and the State Department's ability to meet present and future diplomatic challenges."[92]

CHAPTER 4

Missed Opportunity

In December 2010, the Department of State and the U.S. Agency for International Development released the culmination of two years' effort to outline a vision for the departments that would justify and guide resourcing. The Quadrennial Diplomacy and Development Review was consciously modeled on the Pentagon's Quadrennial Defense Review; Secretary Clinton openly says so in her introduction to the report. The Pentagon is required by law to provide such a review to Congress every four years as part of the 1985 Goldwater-Nichols defense reforms; State has commendably undertaken its review voluntarily, hoping it will produce the benefits DOD has gained from routinely reassessing threats, the current force, future needs, and alignment of spending to those needs.

There is much that is worthwhile in the QDDR: encouraging involvement in foreign policy by civil society beyond the control of the American government; reminding readers of the importance of economic and commercial aspects of diplomacy; acknowledging the need for a new framework for risk management; introducing a circuit rider approach to providing services where full-time staffing is unaffordable; making a commitment to improve its strategy, planning, and evaluation processes; developing multi-year budgets; admitting that State must develop greater expertise to be a valued interagency partner and that "whole-of-government must be more than a mantra"; and acknowledging that the military deserves a stronger partner than State has provided.[1]

The review went mostly unremarked, which is perhaps not surprising given the programmatic nature of the document. DOD's review receives greater attention, but that is because DOD's review has a track record of shaping budgetary decisions, and those decisions affect large economic interests: aerospace and manufacturing, real estate where troops might be moved, etc. The State Department's review, being the first of its kind, has no track record. Reading the document reveals that there is very little effort to connect its vision to budget allocation. And the foreign affairs budget is spent predominantly on the people and operations of the Department of State, with little impact on wider economic activity.

It of course doesn't help that the document is redolent with bureaucratic jargon and risibly airy descriptions, such as the need for diplomats to be "as comfortable in work boots as wing tips," and "whether in pinstripes or cargo pants, (diplomats) are the backbone of America's civilian power," with the ability to "embrace 21st century statecraft," in "plurilateral fora," resulting in civilian power being "the most cost-efficient investment in a time of constrained resources," such that "the lens of civilian power highlights the role of human security in our foreign policy," and exhorting that "leading through civilian power is required by the nature of the problems we face."[2]

But those maudlin descriptions are not the only reason the QDDR has been ignored. Substantively, it has tended to reinforce stereotypes of State as self-congratulatory and programmatically inept. Secretary Clinton claims the question the department asked itself was, "How can we do better?" If so, the answer that rings out from the State Department's first quadrennial review is "by having more money and more senior positions!"

Needless to say, such an answer hardly justifies two years' worth of staff and leadership effort. Nor does it build confidence that State has taken a hard look at where it is deficient—State's performance in the past decade has made clear it is not the peer of the Pentagon in commitment to service, ability to identify and adapt to changing requirements, or building for the future while engaging in demanding activities in the present. The "whole-of-government operations" mantra chanted by Secretary of Defense Robert Gates and Admiral Mullen should be understood as a plea by the Department of Defense for State to better do its job.

Cordesman, one of the most careful readers of DOD's reviews, dismisses the State review as "another vacuous government report calling for clearer lines of responsibility and leadership, more coordination, better strategy, better people, and better planning and management—recommendations that are unquestionably valid in broad terms and meaningless in dealing with urgent, real-world needs in the field."[3]

The review fails to engage several important issues that are essential to an analytically sound basis for the department's budgets. Specifically, it:

★ Asserts the need for more resources, yet never quantifies how much is needed for State and USAID to perform their missions successfully

★ Does not connect the threat assessment to lines of departmental activity

★ Does not prioritize functions or assess resource needs by function

★ Undervalues consular activity, despite it being State's most important function

★ Spends inordinate attention on organizational issues, both internal to State and between State and USAID

★ Does not develop metrics by which performance can be judged (USAID has done a much more creditable job)

The Quadrennial Diplomacy and Development Review will need to become a much more rigorous process for State and USAID to be delivered the money they are seeking and to perform at the level our country needs of them.

We Just Need More

The self-congratulatory feel of the QDDR is summed up in its title, "Leading Through Civilian Power." The department would have been better served not to have selected a title so easily mistaken for an Onion satire of a press release from an underperforming bureaucracy. It is characteristic of the culture of the State Department, though, to assert its titular prerogative rather than merit it on performance.

The Secretary of State is the first cabinet secretary in the line of succession to the presidency. In the 1886 law, precedence was set by the establishment of cabinet department; State being the first cabinet department created, the Secretary of State follows the Speaker of the House in line to the presidency. The Defense Department didn't exist; and if it had, our still young republic would likely have been chary of investing such power in a secretary with the military at his command.

Power has shifted; it had begun to even at the time of the 1886 law.[4] Perhaps that was inevitable, given the settlement of the major diplomatic questions such as demarcation of American territory and admiration accruing to the American military in the Civil War. But in recent decades, the anemic performance of the Department of State has also contributed significantly to the power shift.

The most recent example of State failing to lead through civilian power is illustrative in this regard. In 2005, the State Department was formally given authority by the president to lead stabilization and reconstruction efforts for the U.S. government. No appreciable change has been evident; the military still leads stabilization and reconstruction in the locations where U.S. interests are at stake, most notably Iraq and Afghanistan, even though State has the legal authorities.

As the means of fulfilling State's new role, it created the Office of the Coordinator for Reconstruction and Stabilization (SCRS). Secretary Rice describes the purpose of SCRS as bringing skills that exist in American society into government service, much as the military relies on its Reserve Component for specialized skills:

> We tried three different approaches to nation building: the Balkans were given to the U.N., Afghanistan initially had an 'adopt a ministry' approach, the third was to give it to DOD. The question was how to get whole-of-government action. State doesn't have tax experts, the IRS does. State doesn't have border experts, the INS does. But then you run into tremendous resistance, from those organizations and their congressional oversight committees.
>
> Whole-of-government can only work for very short periods of time, perhaps six weeks, but as a sustained effort, it doesn't work. SCRS was designed to mirror the military's Reserve Component, to bring in people who had a host of civilian functions so that you would have a trained group of civilians who were willing and could be called up for a year or two years to reform judiciary.[5]

Creating a civilian reserve corps that would be called up and deployed to war zones is a thoughtful approach to solving the problem of State's incapacity. State failed to effectively communicate its approach, however, to gain congressional support or to make those capacities functional in the past decade. It also violated the fundamental precept of getting things done in Washington: anything planned for beyond the budget cycle isn't real. State should have built a module of what the office might become and speedily dispatched it to one of the wars so that skeptics could see its value, and on that basis argue for the funding and authority to build on success.

The State Department's explanation for why it has not actually developed civilian power or led efforts at stabilization and reconstruction is instructive: Congress wouldn't give it the money. The department takes very little responsibility for making a set of self-defeating bureaucratic choices that aggravated potential supporters, failing to establish a record of performance that would attract support, and being unwilling to fight for funding inside the administration and with Congress.

The progression of events goes something like this: smarting from being outmaneuvered by Rumsfeld's Pentagon on Iraq, the State Department set about creating a means for early involvement in future crises. Rather than build on USAID's strong record in disaster relief, State established an Office of Stabilization and Reconstruction within State proper. USAID supporters in both the Department and the NGO community viewed this as yet another evisceration of an organization that had been starved of resources and authority by Congress and the State Department for over a decade.

Congress was not persuaded to fund the office, in large part because State never developed a persuasive plan for what the office would accomplish or the required resourcing. The office was nonetheless established with a skeleton staff; it chose to focus its effort on future crises rather than Iraq or Afghanistan. That is, the Office of Reconstruction and Stabilization declined to contribute to the wars the country was fighting, preferring to set its sights on putative future crises.

Ambassadors selected to lead it were not "conflict professionals," people who had served with distinction in societies
that had experienced civil war, famine, or collapse of the state.
When offered staffers from the Pentagon to build the organization, State declined in order to preserve the civilian nature of the
office. Instead of sending a cadre to war zones to organize and
lead civilian partners for the military effort, SCRS remained in
Washington developing charts of civilian reserves who might be
available in several years' time, provided Congress funded the
effort. It became the symbol of State's ineffectualness.

What might State have done instead? It could have utilized
USAID's expertise, enforced discipline at Foggy Bottom in support of the effort when an organizational plan was developed,
selected a prominent diplomat whose career would embody the
ethos of the office being created and with the heft to argue for
resources, and developed a transparent spending program tied
to the achievement of near-term objectives. It could have mobi-
lized non-governmental groups to make the case with Congress
and the public of the importance of funding and conducting the
activity, focused relentlessly on taking charge of stabilization
and reconstruction efforts where they were occurring, shifted
resources from other State/USAID functions to prioritize the new
reconstruction and stabilization mission, and incorporated in the
short term expertise from organizations good at rapidly building
institutional capacity. It could have performed in the war zones
such that other agencies saw the value of SCRS contributions,
committed the White House to legislative vetoes of authoriza-
tion and appropriations vehicles that did not provide funding for
SCRS, had the secretary travel with members of Congress to
inspect the work of SCRS in the field, highlighted the American
interests and communities served by State involvement in this
new mission, celebrated and rewarded the accomplishments
of individual diplomats working bravely in dangerous circumstances, and identified American companies whose exports or

operations were made possible by missions in which SCRS had become involved.

Instead of doing any of these things, State described the importance of what needed doing and bemoaned Congress's failure to provide it with the money and authority to undertake the activity. State is still trying to undo the damage of that stumbling start. The contrast could scarcely be more striking to the way the Department of Defense builds support for activities it considers important and persuades Congress to provide funding.

Meet the New Boss,
Same as the Old Boss

Given the breathless explanations in the QDDR of the changing nature of international power and the multiplicity of groups able to affect American interests, it would be reasonable to expect the review to identify a variety of new tools and practices requiring investment to adapt the Department of State and USAID to this new reality, to give it the capacity to operate successfully and dominate new environments to advance American interests. That is not what the QDDR does, however. Instead, it seeks increased funding for existing obligations and institutional prerogatives.

The Quadrennial Diplomacy and Development Review asks for increased funding in three particular areas: operational funds for dramatically expanded missions in Iraq and Afghanistan; crisis prevention and response; and development. The most crucial problem with the QDDR is that these three areas do not align with the document's description of the international environment, threats to American interests, or even the White House's political objectives. They are the spending requests State would have made had there been no Quadrennial Diplomacy and Development Review.

That the department's first analytic review of activities and resources identified a dramatically changing international environment and concluded that what is needed is materially different only in magnitude, not type, discredits the review. The key analytic challenge of strategic planning is identifying what activities no longer require being done as circumstances change. Technological transformation allows businesses to eliminate tasks that once consumed significant resources; international transformation likewise permits the *not* doing of activity, but the QDDR has not identified anything State or USAID currently does that it will not need to continue doing.

Yet such examples are manifold. The unauthorized release of a quarter million classified diplomatic cables provides a significant data base against which to test the quality of reporting by U.S. diplomatic posts. The good news for American taxpayers is that our diplomats are knowledgeable in the descriptions of what is occurring in the countries in which they are posted. Moreover, they were not revealed to be duplicitous or venal. Overwhelmingly, our diplomats come across as earnestly working with foreign governments to help them succeed at activities in our mutual interest. But the documents yielded few insights, which means all that information was already available to readers of unclassified media. The enormous investment of time and effort in reporting by diplomatic posts is surely less valuable now that information is widely available by non-governmental means. Yet the State Department's QDDR does not consider whether the foundational tasks of diplomacy have been changed by the trends identified in its own report.

All three specific funding requests are problematic and will face difficult passage in Congress. Funding for Iraq faces two difficulties, only one of which is of the State Department's making. The Obama administration has for two years assiduously worked to keep Iraq from being news—positive or negative—and thus

Iraq has faded from public consciousness. The administration did not lead through civilian power in Iraq; in fact, it signally failed to capitalize on the gains won by our military. But it is now seeking $5.2 billion for an expanded diplomatic presence.[6] That will be a difficult sell, with Congress rightly asking why, if the administration didn't care about winning the war, Congress should fund such an elaborate civilian presence.

The second problem in securing expanded funding for State Department operations in Iraq is the weakness of State's plan for operating there after the withdrawal of U.S. military forces in December 2011. State has never managed a program of this magnitude and lacks the skill to build a solid plan of personnel, activities, and funding adequate to the requirements. While highlighting the importance of law enforcement, State has reduced the program because of funding—although, unsurprisingly, it believes reducing effort will not negatively affect the program.[7]

Despite all the assistance proffered by the military in Iraq during 2008–2010 to assist State in developing a transition plan, State's plan is still not executable. To choose a dramatic example: State lacks the ability to transport civilian personnel throughout the country. It plans to rely on contractors to provide transport and protection, including piloting attack helicopters (which State also did not budget for and is now asking DOD to provide gratis).

Increased budget lines for prevention and development both face the difficulty of proving State's assertion that spending for these activities is cost-effective. The QDDR asserts the need to "build our capabilities to prevent and respond to crisis and conflict so as to avoid greater costs down the road" and the value of development for building "strong states and societies that can be our partners in the future."[8] These are bold arguments to make, and smart arguments. They are also, at best, unproven.

Preventive activity is not inherently less expensive than the use of diplomatic, economic, and military tools when a crisis reaches a head. If the country invests in prevention but war nevertheless breaks out, it has incurred a loss of the investment in prevention. If it invests in prevention in a large number of places, none of which fester to crisis, it will be unclear whether those investments were necessary. Some uses of force are cheaper than the costs of non-military tools: investing nothing in prevention and not intervening during a crisis is the cheapest strategy of all.

At a minimum, State ought to have tried to argue the case rather than assert its conclusion. Dwight Eisenhower, who excelled at strategic planning, believed that "plans are useless but planning is everything."[9] What he meant was that the planning process trains the judgment of the people participating in it. And while specific plans may not prove the best approach in a real crisis, the planners will understand the problem better from having been involved in studying practical matters associated with it. By making an intellectually lazy assertion and not bringing more analytic effort to demonstrate the cost-effectiveness of preventive activity, State has deprived its planners of the education of thinking this important issue through, as well as being unpersuasive in its argument for funding.

In the QDDR, State makes an injudicious attempt to contrast the magnitude of spending for defense and diplomacy. For example, the QDDR emphasizes that the entirety of State/USAID funding is equivalent to what DOD currently spends in Iraq. While intended to demonstrate that diplomacy and development are cost-effective, it is more likely to remind Congress how very much the country gets for its defense dollar and to alienate the only solid supporters of increased State budgets outside of State, namely, the Department of Defense.[10]

Development of partner capacity is a major theme of Defense Department planning. By improving the ability of military forces in allied or threatened countries, we reduce the need for use of U.S. military forces. The argument has some wrinkles in the military context (such as providing training to military forces that over-throw their governments, as happened in Latin America so often in the twentieth century, or to national forces that defect to the enemy, as recently occurred in Yemen). It is even more difficult to understand what might be the diplomatic equivalent of strength-ening the capacity for self-defense. Improving customs and law enforcement are surely valuable, but outside the purview of the Department of State. This is likewise true for engagement with the Centers for Disease Control in assisting development of early warning networks with other countries. What is unclear is why those monies would be appropriated through the Department of State, especially given State's remedial programmatic skills. So, as with cost effectiveness, the QDDR's vagueness with respect to its program has failed to make a solid case for funding partner-ship capacity.

State needs to develop considerably more analytic rigor to be persuasive that greater investment is needed in crisis management and improving partner capacity. State's QDDR does not provide a framework by which it can be determined which states (beyond their explicit request for Iraq and Afghanistan) are priorities for attention, what tools State already has available in abundance versus those it needs to acquire, what capabilities partners need that State has the expertise to provide, and what benchmarks could be established to identify progress or its lack.

Rebuilding USAID

Where the QDDR makes its best case for how the changed environ-ment necessitates a different way of doing business is in the USAID chapters of the review. This may be proof of Samuel Johnson's axiom that nothing focuses the mind like a hanging: USAID had until the last few years been subject to significant budget cuts by Congress and now faces competition for its function by the more successful Millennium Challenge Corporation, which excelled at setting standards for its own performance and the performance of governments to which it provides assistance. USAID's leadership has now done a good job critiquing its failures, identifying new approaches to achieve its objectives, and developing metrics by which its own operations and the performance of governments and entities to which it provides funding can be measured. What it has not yet done is answer the fundamental question of how much money needs to be spent on foreign assistance and how much of that amount still needs to be provided by government, given the breadth of private philanthropy.

Congress dramatically cut back funding of the Agency for International Development in the 1990s, intending to fold it back into State, as was done to the Arms Control and Disarmament Agency and the U.S. Information Agency (on the reasonable argument that these are tools of diplomacy and ought to be constituent to the department). USAID managed to escape that subordination, but just barely. It was reduced from an agency that undertook development assistance to an agency that lets contracts for that assistance. USAID often did not help its case with Congress by defending its superior ethos of providing assistance in defiance of American interests or the need to work in concert with the priorities of American foreign policy.

The Bush administration ushered in a revolution by shifting the basis for providing foreign assistance. Instead of focusing on the neediest countries, the administration recalibrated assistance to direct it toward countries that committed to principles of good governance and progress toward self-sufficiency. It is noteworthy that in order to construct this new approach, the administration had to create the Millennium Challenge Corporation; USAID was hostile to the approach, even when it proved successful.

The Obama administration has committed to "elevate development alongside diplomacy and defense as an equal pillar of

American foreign policy."[11] USAID has utilized this opportunity to return from the dead; the strongest and most vibrant parts of the review are those dealing with USAID. While much of the new approach in the President's Directive on Development sounds very much like development policy under President Bush—including the commitment for USAID to put itself out of business by putting countries on a path to self-sustaining progress—USAID has clearly learned to incorporate the attitudes of the Millennium Challenge experiment.[12]

To a much greater degree than the State Department, USAID has thought creatively and is willing to establish criteria for evaluating its own performance. And it cites demonstrable success, noting that "in the latest World Bank Group annual report seven of the 10 top reformers—Kazakhstan, Rwanda, Peru, Vietnam, Tajikistan, Zambia, and Grenada—were USAID partners in working to make it easier for local entrepreneurs to start and expand their businesses."[13]

Nowhere does the State Department summarize its program as well as does USAID:

> . . . we will, first, adopt a new investment strategy that ensures high-impact development by focusing on six areas of comparative U.S. government advantage and by leading Presidential Initiatives in three of these areas. Second, we will build USAID into a world-class development agency through deliberate partnership, innovation, and a focus on results. Third, we will equip USAID with the human capital, the operational and budget oversight capacity, and the institutional voice necessary to transact this new development approach. Finally, we will transform the Department of State to better support our development objectives.

The plan to transform State so that it may better serve USAID's development program is a wonderful and welcome level of ambition. USAID has plans for a development laboratory and a $53 million venture capital fund to support experimental programs that meet standards of a 15 percent return on investment while reaching 75 million people.[14]

And USAID now speaks the language about how its work will have greater resonance beyond the development community. Pulling from the Millennium Challenge approach, it emphasizes "a particular focus on improved tax collection, transparency, and anti-corruption measures. We will do more to promote entrepreneurship. And we will advance a range of measures to capitalize on the value of remittances and other domestic resources for infrastructure development."[15]

The USAID chapter makes clear the United States has interests beyond development in many of our development programs, that economic growth is the most powerful force for eradicating poverty, and that development should advance our national security interests.[16]

It also acknowledges that our assistance programs have problematically relieved governments in developing countries from funding their own public health programs. These will all be welcome admissions to critics of government-funded development assistance.

Moreover, USAID is seeking to become a learning organization, strengthen its technical expertise, energize its employees, build strategic planning capacity, and "reintroduce a culture of research." This is not only good for USAID, it sets a competitive example for State.

In fact, USAID can be said to be the bureaucratic winner of the review. It clawed back significant autonomy, gaining a separate budget from State and a reallocation of State resources to USAID, seizing control over major White House policy initiatives like Feed the Future, gaining authority to chair interagency meetings (rather than have State at the helm), forming its own policy bureau, and even possibly incorporating the

Millennium Challenge Corporation. It has been revivified by developing a new business model emphasizing sustainability and accountability.

Still, it merits noting that all of USAID's plans are stated in the future tense, not the present—they describe what USAID will do, not what it is doing. Pakistan, for example, recipient of $5 billion in U.S. assistance, does not meet the standards USAID outlines in the QDDR. Humanitarian assistance in Haiti after its earthquake is difficult to fit into the agency's rubric. USAID would have made a much stronger case by showing it is actually doing what it describes as its transformational approach.

Moreover, nothing in the QDDR permits establishing how much is enough, either in diplomacy or development. Why is $3.5 billion the right amount for global food aid? How many Foreign Service officers do State and USAID require? The QDDR leaves the answer to these questions uncomfortably close to "however much you will give us." USAID currently has 9,000 employees; why is that the number and why does it require more?

The USAID chapter emphasizes that new donor countries (China, Brazil, Russia) contributed more than $8 billion to development; that the resources of the World Bank have more than quadrupled in the past decade; and that private donors committed more than $52 billion to development assistance. More than 80 percent of U.S. development assistance is non-governmental— it is given by philanthropists and corporations and churches and mosques and synagogues and sister city programs and other outlets of civil society.[17]

This begs the question, never answered in the QDDR, of why U.S. development assistance needs increasing. U.S. development assistance has increased 155 percent in the past decade (from $10 billion in FY 2000 to $26 billion in FY 2010).[18] Is that not adequate, especially with such expansive private giving? And if not, why not?

The QDDR never explains what development assistance needs to be government-based, either. Instead, it emphasizes the need for USAID to coordinate private efforts; this is unpersuasive. The Gates Foundation, currently engaged in a $15 billion effort to improve medical care in poor countries, invests in everything from teacher development to improving crop yields for small farming. These have all traditionally been areas of government assistance. How exactly will USAID coordinate these efforts?

The most significant contribution USAID could make where private philanthropy is concerned would be to serve as a clearinghouse of information about efforts already under way, populations that are underserved by existing efforts, and countries which provide the most conducive environments for external assistance.

Private philanthropy has overwhelmed government foreign assistance by the United States. Yet the QDDR is oddly silent on the marvels made possible by Americans giving their wealth to promote prosperity and health in other places or on any potential concerns about private activity having deleterious foreign policy consequences. The review's description of how the international order is changing emphasizes new and non-governmental actors, but one of the clearest cases of non-governmental activism—in foreign assistance—resulted in no change to the State/USAID resource request.

Failure to Prioritize and Evaluate

The QDDR commits to change the way State does business in four areas, most prominently "adapting to the landscape of 21st century diplomacy" with "issues becoming more interconnected and solutions requiring ever greater cooperation." It identifies seven increasing threats: terrorism, nuclear proliferation, disruptions to the global economy, climate change, cyber attacks, transnational crime, and disease pandemics. These are reasonable enough; where the review is inadequate is tracking from identification of these threats to prioritization of activity for the department.

And truthfully, these trends have been at the forefront of national security thinking for at least a decade. Are we really still explaining that the cold war has ended?[19] While perhaps understandable in the first review of its kind at State, the QDDR discredits itself somewhat by treating as new the very elements it ought to have been grappling with—and has been grappling with—for some time.

Even where the report identifies interesting and important trends, such as the world's largest economies no longer being its richest and therefore development taking on increased importance, the QDDR does not connect its analysis to changes in activity. If developing economies become some of the international system's largest, does that mean we should continue development projects with our economic competitors?

Having diagnosed dramatic changes in the geopolitical landscape, the QDDR commits to having it both ways: "While we increase our engagement with emerging powers and centers of influence, we will also deepen our longstanding U.S. alliances and partnerships—Europe, Asia, and the Middle East—which will remain vital to helping secure and advance U.S. interests."[20] It is the glib "everything is important" feel of the QDDR that makes it of questionable use as a planning document.

Interestingly, the QDDR contains a section on "the national context" in its overview of the geopolitical landscape. Discouragingly, this focuses on the need for increased resources and blandishments of how much more cost-effectively State plans to employ its resources. A sample exhortation is: "it is imperative to recognize that taxpayers' dollars spent on diplomacy and development—even in relatively modest amounts—can and do promote U.S. prosperity and minimize the need for larger expenditures and costs down the road."²¹ These pieties are asserted rather than proven, and therefore unlikely to persuade State's critics.

Even more importantly, State excuses itself from the responsibility of building support in the public and, crucially, on Capitol Hill. State Department officials often bemoan the lack of congressional interest in diplomacy and development, but they never connect that to their salesmanship of the activity. By contrast, DOD matches very carefully the interests of Congress members and their staffs to activities the department is engaged in, provides information on economic and security issues of interest in congressional constituencies, and provides leadership opportunities for members.

The State Department simply does not think creatively about how to involve members of Congress in the activities of the department and how to build members' constituent interests into the program. A country with as rich an immigrant tapestry as ours has natural linkages to practically every country in the globe: Los Angeles is Iran's second largest city, enclaves of immigrants have shaped the history of everywhere from Solvang, California, to Sarasota, Florida. Yet State does not connect Americans with their countries of origin or utilize their talents and success in our foreign policy, much less give members of Congress opportunities to be involved in the policies affecting countries of origin for their constituents. American businesses hire foreign workers and export to foreign markets, and are therefore natural spokeswomen and men for American engagement in the world and policies that foster our exports. Yet State also makes little use of them in the great game of building congressional interest. State acts as though building congressional support for foreign policy is impossible, rather than just difficult.

Another important way the Pentagon succeeds at building congressional confidence that State might consider mimicking is in constructing metrics by which its performance can be assessed. Most of the data on which public analyses of defense policy are conducted comes from the Defense Department itself. Much of it is mandated by congressional reports and testimony requirements, but its provision unquestionably serves DOD's purposes by producing a better informed debate on its policies. When Congress doubted that the surge of forces in Iraq was succeeding, the Pentagon developed an expansive list of criteria on which it then collected data: number of attacks, tips received from Iraqis, hours of power per day, etc. It reported on these factors routinely, so that Congress could track progress and identify failures.

The QDDR explains a number of ways in which the international order is changing, and even identifies practices State will need to adapt; where it falls short is in using those to rebalance efforts by the department and provide assessment tools for itself and others to evaluate its performance. For example, the report describes the speed of information flow, concluding that its responses "must be in real time, with a premium on speed and flexibility."[22] To the Pentagon mentality, that reveals a metric for accountability: establish the speed and flexibility of responses and judge how they change with time, then grade posts' reporting records. Another example is the QDDR's identification of three "new" domains for diplomatic action (leading whole-of-government implementation, reshaping diplomatic ties to regional and global partnerships, and engaging non-state actors), which the QDDR states will become "core missions" of the department. Each of these translates into performance criteria for activity and for the diplomats engaged in them, yet nowhere in the QDDR does it suggest evaluations of diplomats will reflect these new core missions or show how funding will be reallocated to account for their management.

That the Department of State contents itself with exhortation rather than establishing metrics by which it can prove to skeptics that it is doing more with what it has is a major shortcoming of both the QDDR and State's more general approach to the challenge of building confidence in its program. Data are what builds confidence, and State continues to provide too little data to support its claims.

Deck Chairs

Central to the QDDR is the addition of several senior positions in State and USAID. In order to "embrace 21st century statecraft," the department has determined that it requires two additional undersecretaries, a chief economist, a new Bureau for Energy Resources, a Bureau for Counterterrorism, a new Bureau of Conflict and Stabilization Operations, a new deputy assistant secretary for international media support, a Center for Strategic Counterterrorism Information, a Coordinator for Intergovernmental Affairs, and a senior advisor to the secretary for civil society and emerging democracies.

One of the new undersecretaries would be for economic growth, energy, and the environment; the other for civilian security, democracy, and human rights—replacing the assistant secretaries of state (who currently run functional bureaus) for international economics and for democracy, human rights, and labor. The Bureau of Conflict and Stabilization Operations would replace the current Office of the Coordinator for Reconstruction and Stabilization. The Bureau of Counterterrorism would replace the current Office of Counterterrorism. The Civilian Reserve Corps would be replaced "with a more flexible and cost-effective Expert Corps."[23]

The undersecretary for arms control and international security affairs has been determined to need a new Bureau for Arms Control, Verification, and Compliance and a restructuring of the Bureau of International Security and Nonproliferation.[24] Instead of resolving the bureaucratic conflict over stabilization and reconstruction by situating stabilization operations in either State or USAID, the review proposes turning the office into a bureau at State and "strengthening the Office of Transition Initiatives at USAID."[25]

If this sounds like grade inflation, it is. Currently, State has two deputy secretaries, one for policy and the other for resource management. Management has already been increased in stature with the creation of this second deputy secretary for resource management added overtop the undersecretary for management at the beginning of this administration, thus creating a new layer of bureaucracy with the exact same function. Assistant secretaries are now being upgraded to undersecretaries and offices are becoming bureaus. The former assistant secretary for economic, energy, and agricultural affairs, which had one supporting bureau, will become the undersecretary for economic growth, energy, and the environment, with five supporting bureaus. And this arrangement drops an area of central concern to Congress, which is the advancement of markets for American agricultural products.

While reorganization of the department is probably overdue, State has suffered from an inability to prioritize both threats and departmental resources; relabeling existing functions seems unlikely to produce leadership focus and gives the unwelcome perception that State is merely creating more senior positions for itself. The QDDR's recommended reorganization would be much more credible if it had identified functions that have diminished in importance as well as additional priorities.

The QDDR spends much less attention on improving the department's expertise in the areas identified as newly important. Geo-economics training will now be required for some diplomats (those in the "political cone"), but this falls far short of what would produce an integral understanding of economics consistent with the report's conclusion that "the most powerful tools may be economic." The review has added bureaus in areas, such as sanctions, where the expertise resides elsewhere; in the case of sanctions, it is the Department of the Treasury that has excelled, not the State Department.

The same holds true for State's creation of a Bureau of Arms Control, Verification, and Compliance. That expertise is well-established in the intelligence community, both military and civilian. What will State contribute that is not already under way? Its claim is that "verification and compliance regimes are built into arms control agreements from their inception and that compliance with all such agreements is diligently verified," but that is clearly already done.[26]

A similarly discouraging note comes in the QDDR's top recommendation for strengthening multilateral diplomacy and international institutions, which is to strengthen its own bureau handling these issues.[27]

Reshuffling the deck of State's offices became the focus of the QDDR's evaluation of functions, ignoring the more important question of what expertise is essentially resident in State and what State should capitalize on from other departments.

Power Grab

Other agencies are extremely skeptical of placing State at the head of their operations, either in Washington policymaking or abroad. Just to take one example, the FBI is unlikely to accept diplomatic oversight of investigations its agents are conducting in countries like Yemen. Yet the QDDR asserts that "our Ambassadors will have to direct and coordinate global civilian operations in the field and pursue diplomatic initiatives that involve many disparate parts of the U.S. government."[28]

Moreover, the review's top personnel recommendation—the foremost of all changes to improve the investment in the people of the Department of State—is to "ensure that U.S. government personnel understand and internalize their accountability to the Chief of Mission."[29]

The review recommends the ambassador be given input into the performance evaluation of employees from other agencies, to reinforce unity of purpose at embassies—but of course does not suggest the ambassador be evaluated by other agency personnel to reflect whether the ambassador is serving those agencies' functions well.[30]

There is not unity of purpose at embassies, nor do ambassadors often have the expertise to evaluate staff. For example, in the Bush administration, the ambassador to the Court of Saint James—Great Britain—was a political ally of the president. By profession, he was a breeder of thoroughbred horses. It is difficult to see how that ambassador would be fit, especially in his first year of service, to grade the performance of an intelligence operative in the embassy who was handling coordination of clandestine intervention in Lebanon, or of a military officer involved in bilateral nuclear weapons programs, or of a Department of Agriculture staffer working on scientific scoring of genetically modified grains. State fears its ambassadors becoming figureheads at embassies they do not control. But it will not prevent that outcome by asserting authority; State will only gain authority by adding value to the work that is being done by other agencies.

Instead of attempting to control activity through the Chief of Mission, State should see itself as providing the legal authority for activity actually conducted by other government agencies. Colonel Michael Meese, who was one of the senior military staff involved in coordinating whole-of-government operations in Afghanistan, points to State misconstruing its role:

> The State Department culture that focused on observing, reporting, and then conducting diplomacy does not usually have expertise in (and is therefore not very good at) the project

management and capacity building actions that are necessary
in a post-conflict environment. In most cases, the people with
the capacity to do it and the project management culture to
do it are likely those people who do that in other agencies of
our government. But State has the legal authority overseas.
What State ought to do is become the general contractor, who
does understand the overall legal authorities, and within that
they ought not control the implementation, but they ought to
be able to trust the professionals from the US government or
whoever else is carrying out the activity.[31]

The QDDR's second recommendation is an expanded role for
the ambassador in Washington policymaking. That is, in addition to the Department of State serving as the conduit for diplomats and providing their input, deployed diplomats should be
directly involved. The QDDR does commit to enhanced training
of both career and politically appointed ambassadors, but only
generically—"we will ensure that new Ambassadors receive sufficient training to fulfill their mission and responsibilities," with
no attempt to identify what training would be required or how it
will be enforced on the half of all ambassadors who are political
appointees of an incoming president.[32]

The QDDR seeks to allay concerns about the ambassador as
CEO of all activity in a country. It acknowledges that "State and
USAID's ability to advance our national security interests rests not
on asserted authority but on competence, knowledge, expertise,
impact, and ability and willingness to collaborate."[33] Yet the QDDR
proceeds to assert that authority without developing a program to
justify it. The QDDR does not provide guidance for acquiring that
competence or squaring an expanded authority for ambassadors
with the growing needs of other government agencies.

This is an important area and a genuinely difficult problem,
one not amenable to broad assertions of authority not underwrit-
ten by competence. Probably the best that can practically be done

in improving the quality of interagency coordination at embassies is leaving wide latitude to capitalize on the skills of ambassadors who prove to be good managers of diverse activity while compensating from Washington for those who do not.

The Mission

A crucial part of any institutional review like the QDDR is defining the institution's mission. For the Department of State it is especially important, because the expanded functions of other government agencies really do call into question the balance of expertise and authority given to diplomats rather than funneled through embassies from other departments. A clear mission statement would permit separating out that which State must undertake and that which occurs at embassies but is the purview of the departments of Justice, Defense, Agriculture, Homeland Security, and the other dozens of other agencies represented in U.S. embassies. A clear mission statement would assist Congress in determining where money should be provided in State's budget rather than the budgets of the agencies actually performing the work. For example, to what extent does State need expertise in economics rather than better relying on the expertise in the Department of Treasury, the National Economic Council, the Export Import Bank, and the Office of the U.S. Trade Representative?

State's review identifies five core civilian missions:

★ Prevent, resolve, and end conflicts

★ Counter threats that cannot be addressed through U.S. military force alone

★ Address and solve global political, economic, and security problems that directly affect the United States and cannot be solved by the United States alone

★ Advance a positive U.S. political, economic, development, environmental, and values agenda in the world

★ Connect Americans to the world and the world to America by assisting American citizens who travel and live abroad while serving as the front line of our border security

These are reasonable objectives, although they are insufficiently distinct for planning purposes. Whittling the blowsiness out of the description ("connect Americans to the world and the world to Americans") would have better served understanding. Presumably in claiming to be "the front line of our border security," the Department of State means its consular services of issuing visas for travel by foreigners to the United States and being a link to their government for Americans outside our country. These are both hugely important functions—arguably the most important tasks American diplomats perform—yet they are lumped together at the bottom of State's list.

It is an insight into the culture of the State Department that it begins with the grand internationalism it does to least effect and which has the least direct application to the lives and well-being of the American people. This tells us what State Department officials most value of their work. Yet the core diplomatic missions would resonate more with Congress if they began with the functions that have the greatest direct resonance on American lives: preventing dangerous people from entering the United States and ensuring Americans abroad have a means of connecting to their government's protection. Assisting in the division of Sudan into two countries is a laudable role for American diplomats; preventing terrorists from getting visas to board airplanes to Detroit is of understandably greater interest to the taxpaying public.

The QDDR does a better job in the body of the report, listing the mission of the department as "advancing four fundamental

national interests: protecting the security of the United States and
its citizens, allies and partners; promoting prosperity at home
and abroad with a strong U.S. economy and an open international economic system that promotes opportunity; supporting
the spread of universal values; and shaping a just and sustainable
international order that promotes peace, security, and opportunity through cooperation to meet global challenges."[34] Needless to
say, that the report contains differing descriptions of the department's core missions is unhelpful.

In speaking of the grand functions of diplomacy—preventing
wars and addressing global problems—the QDDR too often treats
as new phenomena things it should already have adapted to. So,
for example, the emphasis on networks and non-governmental
organizations sounds a decade behind recognition of those problems in both academic and defense circles. And the rhetoric has
too little meaning: what are the threats that the military cannot
solve alone? How do they differ from preventing and resolving
conflicts or global problems? A simplification and recasting of
State's core functions could go something like this:

★ Protect the United States by screening foreigners seeking to
   come to our country

★ Assist Americans when they are abroad

★ Promote American interests, values, and policies

★ Work with other governments to solve problems threatening
   the well-being of Americans

★ Work with other governments and international organizations
   to strengthen their ability to solve their problems, thereby
   reducing the need for American involvement

★ Create opportunities for American business

These are not delicate diplomatic descriptions; they are objectives around which to organize plans. They exclude many virtuous activities our diplomats engage in, and they are stringent in their focus on the good of the United States rather than the entire world. But in their directness, they permit prioritization of effort, which is essential to good planning. They allow diplomats to sift which problems to solve and where to focus their efforts.

While the QDDR was being written, State's performance of each of those objectives was in the news. The salience of the report would have been increased if State had included case studies that analyzed what diplomats had done well and poorly. Sadly, the culture of the State Department is not attuned to the importance of after-action reviews that roughly critique performance in order to teach improved performance. Such analyses are seen as unduly critical of diplomats trying hard in difficult circumstances and without adequate resources or support.

State missed the opportunity of giving us an education on the often boring but critical work of consular affairs; portraits of the predominantly young diplomats on whose judgment those decisions rest and who perform that work with a very high degree of success; analysis of whether we have the right number of officers needed for that work; weaknesses of the system that have been identified and have since been improved; and the equipment, training, and processes that will enhance the safety of Americans in the future.

The Quadrennial Diplomacy and Development Review would also be a more valuable document if, having identified the principal functions of its work, State then organized the remainder of the report in lines of activity those objectives required, justifying resourcing for the overall budget by analyzing what will be needed to continue performing those functions well.

Conflict Management

Instead of that careful plotting of objectives to resources, the QDDR seeks to justify a widely expanded role in a mission State has nominally been in charge of since 2005: conflict management. The QDDR rightly highlights the problems of failing states, and this is the only section of the review that engages in even once-over-lightly self-criticism. Yet even in identifying ten reasons State has underperformed in the area of conflict management, the review's central explanation is that State "react(s) to each successive conflict or crisis by reinventing the process for identifying agency leadership, establishing task forces, and planning and coordinating U.S. government agencies."[35] To translate, that means State Department officials assess their failure to perform this crucial function well as the result of not being able to figure out how to work with others to perform mission-critical and time-sensitive work . . . yet they believe they should lead the interagency process.

The QDDR even states that "many of the capabilities and skills we need for conflict and crisis prevention and response exist at State, USAID, and other federal agencies, but these capabilities are not integrated and focused on the problem in a sustained way."[36] That is, we have the ability to undertake this work, we just haven't. The QDDR is describing a problem set that has been the norm of American diplomatic activity for two decades and for which State has had explicit presidential authority to lead since 2005. Yet the institution has not adapted to succeed at a task it considers crucial.

Contrast that with the way the American military innovated during the wars in Iraq: the threats that rapidly developed in Iraq were not anticipated by military or civilian planners (although they should have been), but the organization moved within the space of a couple of years to analyze the threats, experiment with alternative approaches, develop doctrine from the most success- ful of those approaches, and dramatically change its strategy and operations to succeed. There is no State Department counterpart to the intellectual and operational revolution of counterinsur- gency theory in the military.[37]

If State could develop a culture of evaluation and adaptation, its assertions of leadership would be much more plausible. In fact, we have an overall test for the quality of State performance: it is the migration of fundamentally civilian tasks to the military, which continues apace despite nearly ten years of increases in State and USAID funding.

The Review does get the conflict prevention and management mission right:

> . . . temporary order and an end to violence can usually be established through the application of force, the civilian mission is one of preventing conflict, saving lives, and building sustainable peace by resolving underlying grievances at both the individual and community levels and helping to build government institutions that can provide basic but effective security and justice. Over the longer term, the core of the mission is to build a government's ability to address challenges, resolve conflicts, promote development and provide for its people on its own."[38]

The QDDR includes a long list of the resources State and USAID bring to this problem set, but then claims nothing more can be done without additional resources. It properly high- lights that the department's capacity in conflict management is the excellence of the individuals engaged in the activity, not the institutional support provided by State toward the activity, but then it concludes State cannot do more without additional fund- ing. It emphasizes the importance of security and justice sector reform, but does not explain what is needed to do that work successfully. USAID allocates only 25 percent of its assistance to the thirty countries it classifies as the highest risk for conflict and instability.[39]

That budget allocation conveys the actual importance the organization ascribes to the activity. Moreover, USAID does not outline the means by which it decides when and where development assistance ought to coincide with conflict prevention and management.

Given State's performance in the area of conflict management, it would have been a much smarter approach to prioritize existing resources to the mission, set performance criteria by which it could be held accountable, and only subsequently seek additional funds once it has proven its concept of operations. State would have built confidence among stakeholders—congressional funders and interagency partners—if it had used the significant resources already in its control to improve its performance at what it considers a core mission.

State and USAID also undercut confidence in their seriousness about the conflict management mission by devoting effort to justifying the need for an "international operational response framework," suggesting yet another solipsistic bureaucratic exercise to undertake that which should already be under way. Here is the QDDR description:

> State and USAID will coordinate with interagency partners, through the National Security Staff led process, to develop an International Operational Response Framework that establishes the systems and procedures necessary to ensure transparent and accountable leadership structures and agency lines of responsibility which, when combined, will leverage and deliver the full range of U.S. international disaster, crisis, and conflict response resources. . . . In developing this new framework, State and USAID will conduct a fact-based

analysis of past failures and successes in interagency response mechanisms, both international and domestic, to determine what works.

Green-Colored Glasses

The Department of State and USAID suffer from too little programmatic proficiency. Fighting commanders always complain about tedious accountants expecting them to keep track of what is being done. The Duke of Wellington is widely (if possibly apocryphally) quoted complaining to Whitehall that he could either keep careful inventory of jars of jam or else defeat Napoleon, and the British Foreign Office should instruct him as to which. But the accountability for spending that drives programmatic oversight is the wellspring from which budgetary credibility results. State is not trusted with money because it has weak accounting oversight and opaque methods of determining needed expenses.

Secretary Rice recounts amazement at asking the State Department's budget officers to show her how much money was being spent on the president's priority of advancing democracy and being told there was no means of determining that. She concluded ". . . these budget reviews were just horrendous, they weren't management reviews. The budget is a management tool, but the State Department budget was a bunch of accounts that didn't relate to programs."[40]

The Quadrennial Diplomacy and Development Review admirably contains a section on the need for management reform, beginning with an admission that current planning processes "require too much staff time . . . and provide too little analytical information in return."[41] This is a promising start and should be built upon as the means of persuading Congress that State's budget is both necessary and well-spent. Instead of arguing, as it now does, that it requires more money to do its work well, State should reverse the arrow and show what it is able to do well as the basis for arguing for budget increases.

State has vacillated between giving embassies and missions wide latitude and developing a process that channels funding to the secretary's priorities. A major stumbling block in the process of the organization's leader directing its resources has been the cultural proclivity on the part of members of the Foreign Service and civil service at State and USAID to consider themselves bulwarks against American foreign policy being too much affected by politics.

A noble goal, it would seem, except that the politicization they believe they have a responsibility to prevent is otherwise known as accountability to elected officials. The president has both a right and a responsibility to shape America's foreign commitments and policies consistent with her or his campaign platform. Yet many of the professionals at Foggy Bottom really do consider themselves above the grubby confines of democratic politics where foreign policy is concerned. This attitude shocks the sensibilities of people acclimatized to the American military, and would never be tolerated were it displayed by people wearing uniforms instead of suits. It may also explain State's difficulty in engaging with Congress.

Disappointingly, the management chapter is the most vacuous part of the QDDR. It commits to "elevate and improve strategic planning," "align budgets to planning," and develop a flow of guidance documents beginning with a Joint Strategic Plan that cascades into priorities guidance and integrated country strategies, and from which are developed multiyear budgets.[42] It even commits to "transition to integrated national security budgeting" (something the president has not even proposed). These are all virtuous objectives, but the fact remains that State has worked two years under the current leadership without going beyond such a description to establishing any of these systems that would produce desired results.

In the year since the QDDR was released, none of these systems have been put into place. The secretary has not signed directives realigning the planning and budgeting process. This may partly be due to Deputy Secretary Jacob Lew departing to become the director of the President's Office of Management and Budget. But if so, making a central component of reform so dependent on a single person is a basic managerial mistake within the secretary's power to correct.

State describes a proposed process rather than putting systems into place that develop habits of programming oversight. There is, for example, no discussion of the physical platform of embassies, whether they are sized and staffed appropriately to their purposes, and what alternatives might be experimented with, except for a vague reference to risk management.

The QDDR is right to highlight that a central purpose of the planning process will be to provide better justification for budgets.[43] But that will require building skills to analyze requirements, track resources to priorities, and assess outcomes. It bodes ill that what State describes as its two major accomplishments in strategic planning are the appointment of a deputy secretary responsible for the function and a "streamlining" of reports it will provide to Congress.[44]

The QDDR's program for personnel management illustrates just how far State has to go before it has the programmatic proficiency to manage its resources well and build confidence on Capitol Hill that it merits continued increases in funding. State says the right kinds of things in the Quadrennial Review: ". . . we will change the way we award, manage, and monitor contracts to ensure that inherently governmental functions are carried out by government personnel."[45] Unfortunately, this pledge is at wide variance with State's practice, most tellingly in the war zones of Iraq and Afghanistan.

State also makes disingenuous claims about its personnel requirements. For example, in speaking about Iraq, Pakistan, and Afghanistan, the QDDR states that "from 2006 to 2010 we have nearly doubled the numbers of employees reporting to the Chiefs of Mission in these three countries from almost 2,600 to more than 5,000. By 2012 we expect that number to rise to 6,396." Yet its own chart shows that State Department staff—Foreign Service officers and civil servants—will have only increased by 334 in Iraq, Pakistan, and Afghanistan across the Obama administration's "civilian surge."[46] The preponderant change is not in State Department employees but in other civilian government departments and contractors.

Even as it makes its case that it is dramatically understaffed, State demonstrates its inability to manage personnel to priorities. One in six Foreign Service positions worldwide is unfilled— that is, State is tolerating a 17 percent gap between existing manpower requirements and its labor force. It has not asked of Congress the funding to remediate this chasm, nor has it identified positions to take off the books knowing it will not have the resources to fill them. Instead, State allows positions to remain unfilled, hoping the shortfalls will induce Congress unbidden to provide for them.

State Department officials fail the basic managerial test of balancing resources and requirements: instead of calculating what is needed and making their case for it, they simply argue for more. The QDDR admits State lacks the ability to even track expertise in its current workforce.[47] An increase of nearly 50 percent in the Foreign Service since 2001 has not decreased the rate of unfilled positions; State has instead increased staffing requirements.

A Starting Point

Before the QDDR there already existed a substantial wealth of solid recommendations for improving State's performance: the 2007 *Embassy of the Future* report and the 2006 *Smart Power* report, both by the Center for Strategic and International Studies; the American Academy of Diplomacy report on education and the Stimson Center report, *A Foreign Affairs Budget for the Future*, are also noteworthy. Most of these go further than the QDDR and also assign cost figures to their recommendations. If State in the past two years had undertaken any of the proposed activities with vigor instead of describing what it will do, American diplomacy would have a reasonable claim to lead through civilian power.

State missed an enormous opportunity to turn a self-critical eye on its own performance and to undertake a more substantive assessment of its requirements and capacities. In doing so it sacrificed much of the credibility it needs to justify its call for major increases in funding. Yet even though it underperforms several other external efforts, the review served three important purposes: educating the new administration team, focusing the department on the secretary's priorities, and giving Congress a baseline against which to judge subsequent budget requests.

First, the QDDR served to teach the new political appointees about the department they are engaged to run. Most senior political appointees, in State as elsewhere in government, have little experience in the departments they are appointed to, and where they do have experience it is often nearly a decade out of practice. Our system of political appointments, so enriching by bringing fresh ideas and a commitment to the elected leadership's agenda, makes us a government of amateurs. One important function quadrennial reviews serve is to bring the new appointees up to speed on what is actually being done and on what money is actually being spent in their department.

A second important function of quadrennial reviews in the Defense Department is that they bring the members of the department together to reaffirm the purposes of their work. Staffing the review is an enormous undertaking, with different parts of the organization seeking to defend their priorities and budgets. In DOD, the review process commences more than a year before the review itself, as military services and defense agencies build their teams to advocate their interests. Good reviews set clear priorities and align spending to them—there are clear winners and losers as the secretary establishes a vision for the department. State's initial QDDR is less likely to serve this purpose, partly because the culture of the department is less disciplined than the command culture of the military and partly because there do not appear to be significant budgetary trade-offs outlined in the review. There is no comparable trade-off in the QDDR to Secretary Gates' judgment in the 2008 QDR to prepare for counter-insurgencies rather than large-scale armor battles and to focus on near-term threats rather than optimize the defense program to the longer-term rise of peer-competitors.

The third function served by quadrennial reviews is to provide a program by which Congress can grade the department's subsequent spending choices. The first two purposes of the review process are internally focused; this third shifts focus out to those who oversee the work of the department. Congress gets to grade the department's work: How well have they described the nature of challenges? How seriously have they thought about alternative approaches? How much analytic rigor have they brought to building their budget? How closely does their budget track with their stated priorities? To use a specific example from this QDDR, it calls for "an affirmative American agenda— a global agenda—that is uncompromising in its defense of our security but equally committed to advancing our prosperity and standing up for our values."[48] Congress can and should use that standard to assess the performance of the Obama administration's policies.

Such oversight is not only essential in a democracy, it builds confidence on Capitol Hill that the department is spending its money well. This purpose is even more important for State than for DOD, which already largely has the confidence of Congress on programmatic issues. For State, the review process is a crucial means by which it can show an understandably skeptical Congress that it is developing better budgetary skills. State needs to pass the green-eyeshade test of developing a long-term budget process that will give Congress greater confidence it is spending taxpayers' money well. The current QDDR still looks at the world through rose-colored glasses.

The unfortunate truth is that having taken two full years to develop a strategic plan for the department, the secretary is left with little time to achieve it. Setting a vision halfway through a president's term encourages opponents to wait for a different secretary and a different vision. And the reception of this Quadrennial Diplomacy and Development Review would have been very different in the 111th Congress, with its Democratic majority of the same party as the president, than it will be in the 112th Congress, which has different priorities.[49]

What is needed now is to develop a means for making the Quadrennial Diplomacy and Development Review a more rigorous review of areas for improvement and a more substantive analysis of the specific resources that will bring the Department of State and the U.S. Agency for International Development up to the standard of performance at which the American military operates.

CHAPTER 5

Possibilities

Earlier chapters of this book have been caustic in their evaluation of the State Department's culture, plans, and programs. The goal was to turn a harsh light on the department, to abrade away what President Bush in a different context called "the soft bigotry of low expectations," and to hold the Department of State to the same exacting standards to which we hold the Pentagon.

We deserve, the Department of State deserves, and the country urgently needs for our diplomatic corps to genuinely become the peer of its military counterparts. The department needs the leadership attention, sustained funding, skilled people, programs, and institutional commitment that will set them up for success. Important changes are under way, largely the result of actuarial tables—of hiring a wave of new diplomats who have chosen to serve their country in time of war and who have a different approach to the practice of diplomacy and the risks associated with that practice.

But individual excellence is not enough. If it were, the good people who already excel in our diplomatic corps would have made it successful. What is needed is construction of the institutional bases for success: the programs and practices that craft an entrepreneurial, learning culture and strengthen it by the bureaucratic functioning of the organization. Also necessary is attention by senior leadership to make the institution a means of improving individual performance. What follows is a vision of what that State Department might look like.

Vision

Often ridiculed as business school alchemy, establishing a vision assists an organization to identify a common goal. It provides a clear image of the future state in order to guide disparate effort and motivate people in the organization. An assessment process ought to include the organization's leadership; identify critical tasks; assess the competencies, motives, and demographics of its people; and provide an understanding of both the formal organization and its culture.[1]

The process is especially important for an organization like the State Department, which suffers from several problems: a leadership team that is generally inexperienced in the organization's functions; a poor match between its people and the skills needed to perform critical tasks; a formal organization that does not measure and reward activity identified as crucial; and a strong organizational culture resistant to change. This is the role a Quadrennial Diplomacy and Development Review should play.

Quickly walking through a simple model for implementing strategic change in organizations, State could craft a positive vision to unite the Foreign Service and the civil service with the political leadership and identify where to focus the institution's efforts. It would immediately identify the performance gap between what State does and what needs doing.

The State Department's Foreign Service and civil service members excel at reporting on what's happening in the countries where they're posted and at smoothing over disagreements— what's called minimizing disturbances in bilateral relations.[2] Yet these are no longer the critical tasks of American diplomacy. What is needed from American diplomats are five fundamental activities:

1. Advocating on behalf of Americans and our interests abroad

2. Providing information which is essential to decisions but is otherwise unavailable

3. Assessing the consequences of events and policies under consideration

4. Developing strategies for implementing policies and carrying them out once decided

5. Coordinating the work of agencies in foreign countries

The first task remains unchanged. The second, third and fourth tasks all have their roots in State's culture of observation and reporting, but allow better filtering of information to reduce reporting quantity and place a greater emphasis on analysis and implementation than State does.

State does not currently have the knowledge and skills to perform these tasks.[3] Its people are smart and adaptive, but untrained and given little responsibility. Moreover, the institution of the State Department does not measure or reward employees' performance in these terms. As organizations usually get what they measure and reward, the culture and informal structure of the State Department resists the activities necessary for these critical tasks to be performed.[4]

A vision that might better align the organization's needs with the incentives for its people would reward improving the skills of the Foreign Service and civil service, encouraging a positive attitude toward change. It would acknowledge the problem of State functions migrating to other agencies and give a reason or reasons to prefer State as the locus of activity. It might go something like this:

> The Department of State will become the agency of choice for promoting American interests abroad by providing high-quality analysis and low-cost implementation of policies. Our people will be second to none in their knowledge of how governments operate and how to work effectively in other societies, and will use that expertise to coordinate the work of other U.S. government agencies abroad.

Mission and Functions

The Department of State exists first and foremost to protect Americans. Outside the United States, that entails ensuring American citizens are treated by foreign governments with due processes internationally agreed upon: the embassy must be notified when Americans are taken into custody and be allowed access to them. The embassy supervises any criminal or judicial proceedings and provides information to other U.S. government agencies and to families. The embassy is also responsible for getting information to known Americans within a country when dangerous circumstances develop, whether natural or man-made, and facilitating evacuation when necessary. These basic consular activities are the principal function of American diplomats abroad, the reason that diplomats still need to be posted overseas in an age of globalized communication.

Inside American territory, the State Department still has a vital role to play in protecting Americans, because it issues visas to foreign nationals to enter the United States. In deciding who to permit entry, State is the first line of defense in an age of frequent travel, interconnected economies, and labor mobility. The United States attracts four times more immigrants than any other country.[5] Our civic peace, religious freedom, job opportunities, universities, and many other attractions are magnetic, bringing America some of the world's most talented and motivated people and enriching our country.

The flip side is also true: some of the world's most dangerous people would seek to damage the United States. It is a principal function of the Department of State to determine which applicants are which, and to prevent those who would harm Americans in America from having access to our territory. This is not the State Department's job alone, obviously; the Citizenship and Immigration Services, Customs and Border Protection, Federal Bureau of Investigation, National Counterterrorism Center, Homeland Security, and other agencies all have roles in a layered defense to protect us. But State is the principal conduit and the first line of defense since most foreigners visit American embassies to apply for visas to travel, study, or work in the United States.

While consular work is not the work State values about itself, it is the work taxpayers and Congress value most. The State Department is rarely held accountable for failure of a multilateral negotiation (that blame tends to accrue to the White House for the policy rather than to State for the artistry or effectiveness of its negotiating), but is absolutely held responsible when someone is provided a visa to the United States who turns out to be a threat. State is even blamed for having information that other agencies could have utilized to identify or apprehend potential threats.

It is America's diplomats who check law enforcement and immigration data bases for information that would disqualify a visa applicant. It is America's diplomats who interview visa candidates and make a judgment whether their claims for asylum are valid, whether their documentation for schools or jobs is legitimate, and whether their protestations of family living in the United States are genuine. All this is accomplished by 1,435 people whose salaries are funded by fee collections from visa applicants.[6]

The sifting process is not just negative. Diplomats must also create opportunities for foreigners who would strengthen American society and the American economy by seeking out scholars whose research could be furthered by collaboration with American scholars and learning communities; entrepreneurs whose ideas and tenacity will foster economic growth and spur domestic innovation; and religious leaders who provide the moral beacons which strengthen their communities and ours. Identifying these people, engaging with their activities, and developing relationships that result in opportunity for common cause are also core diplomatic functions for the United States.

From 93 to 95 percent of all foreigners who come into an American embassy are seeking consular assistance.[7] The important work of determining which of them can be admitted to our country is principally undertaken by our most junior diplomats. Typically, consular work is the first tour of all new Foreign Service officers and the specialization of last resort as they select a "cone" of activity. Just as top-notch military pilots typically choose fighter planes, with descending choice of bombers and then tankers or cargo aircraft, diplomats choose political issues, then economic, and finally consular as the functional specialties for their careers.

Americans should be grateful that our diplomats are overwhelmingly right in their judgments about visa applications. Yet our diplomats are not always right in their judgments, as the Christmas 2009 bombing attempt frighteningly demonstrates. Umar Farouk Abdulmutallab received a visa for travel to the United States despite his father having reported him to State Department personnel in Nigeria as dangerously radicalized and involved with extremists in Yemen. The State Department had the information, performed the necessary screening, but misspelled his name and therefore did not access the information. As a result, Abdulmutallab's visa was not revoked nor was he placed in the terrorist screening database or "no-fly" list. These were failures of enormous significance, nearly deadly for 290 people, in no way minimized by the fact that a clerical error was the root cause.

The ease with which Abdulmutallab slipped through the system should be as alarming to diplomats as to intelligence professionals. The consular officer did not check by passport number for Abdulmutallab's visa, relied on the intelligence community's assessment rather than applying any reasoning of his own to the Abdulmutallab file, and, although in possession of information that the applicant was involved with Yemeni extremists, did not add Abdulmutallab to any of the watch lists.[8] National Intelligence Director Dennis Blair resigned in the aftermath, but there were no repercussions in the Department of State, which is arguably the agency most responsible for the intelligence failure, because it was in possession of the information and in control of the visa process.

The State Department should be challenged—required—to improve both its training and its systems for preventing terrorist suspects from gaining admission to the United States. It should be pressed into a major information technology upgrade that will increase confidence the system is accessing the full range of relevant information. The workload of consular officials should be investigated to determine if fatigue or burnout compromises their judgment. Personnel slots should be routinely reevaluated for consular officers in countries with high rates of suspect visa applicants to ensure diplomats have adequate skills and support to continue making good judgments. Standards for consular officers should be established that reward independent judgment, balance risk and reward in awarding visas, and provide information to the intelligence community to allow analysts to better construct threat portfolios. Consular officials should receive additional training to heighten their proficiency at not only information collection and dissemination, but also judgment in difficult cases; these will always be judgment calls, therefore training materials should be developed and training time allotted so that diplomats study cases and evaluate historically significant choices. Diplomats who prove especially good at consular work should be provided with incentives to remain engaged in it rather than proceeding to other "cones" of department activity.

By not elevating the role of consular activity in its analysis of staffing needs and public outreach, the Department of State is missing an enormous opportunity to both do its job better and gain the recognition and funding it seeks. State has estimated that our largest twenty embassies will double their consular workload within two years. Yet, its hiring tables do not reflect a proportionate expansion of consular staff to address that anticipated increase.[9] Nor has State provided data to allow outside analysis of this estimate. Creating a metric that allows leveling of workloads across functional areas and across embassies could establish a baseline, and from that baseline State staffing levels could be established to better align workloads with the importance of consular work.

Within the State Department, the fact that consular work is undertaken predominantly by the most junior diplomats and by those least competitive with their peers among more senior diplomats creates a negative association with the activity. In order to raise the value accorded consular activity, more senior diplomats and more diplomats from outside the consular "cone" should be folded into the staffing mix. They could either be assigned on a full-time basis or have a consular component to even high-profile policy jobs so that the elite are connected to the trenches, so to speak.

In full-time assignment, presumably the work will not be as substantively challenging as other assignments, but that could be compensated for by having those assignments come after hardship posts or extraordinarily demanding and time-consuming policy positions. They could also be made more interesting and rewarding to more senior and non-consular diplomats by utilizing that time also for education and for formal mentoring of junior diplomats. The vision would be to have consular tours encouraged for all Foreign Service officers several times in their careers so that experienced diplomats and those new to the profession work together and are provided the time and opportunity for professional development.

Reshaping the Foreign Service around the principal functionality of consular service is a radical idea. But the changing technological, communications, and political landscape suggests that many functions traditionally undertaken by diplomats abroad are no longer as necessary as they once were. Other means are available for acquiring information. Diplomats are often not well equipped (both literally and figuratively) to provide information and shape foreign government thinking and activity on areas of crucial economic and political importance. Also, many activities that were once the provenance of diplomacy are now run from the White House or other agencies.

Consular activity is the bricks-and-mortar work of diplomacy, and it is difficult to see ways it could cease to be so. State is currently experimenting with video interviews for visa applicants, but it will be difficult to persuade Congress and the public of an acceptable substitute for in-person evaluations. When Americans living or traveling abroad are in danger, they will also want the reassurance of a person rather than a call center to help solve their problems. For Americans taken into foreign custody, there is no substitute for a diplomat routinely checking whether governments have apprehended Americans and are treating them according to international convention.

The State Department has a real opportunity to showcase its success in consular affairs, identify ways to improve performance, and request Congress to provide the resources necessary to improve both the systems and the people utilizing them. The Christmas bombing attempt gives the State Department a rare opening to rethink how it performs consular activity and what kinds of increased investment in people and infrastructure would make it even more successful. Practically the entire hiring cohort Secretary Clinton seeks in Diplomacy 3.0 could be justified by decreasing workload; increasing training and education; and establishing and working to higher standards of performance in consular affairs.

If State does not take up that challenge (and there is little evidence it is doing so), Congress should impose it. State must be held accountable for performing exceptionally well the function of greatest importance to Americans; all other functions should be subordinated to the success of protecting Americans at home and abroad.

The Right Stuff

The State Department acknowledges in the QDDR that our diplomats are deficient in several skill sets at the core of diplomacy as currently practiced. It notes that "the range of global challenges we face also requires much more specialized expertise, and the pace of change and modes of doing business in an interconnected world require a greater ability to innovate, experiment, and work with a wide range of partners."[10] The department even acknowledges "specific new skills and knowledge sets State needs to address the challenges of our increasingly complex world: familiarity with new technology; scientific training; security sector and rule of law experience; expertise in humanitarian assistance, gender issues, energy security, environmental issues, and macroeconomics; among others."[11] What State does not seem to acknowledge is that its model of hiring and professional development does not produce either the skills or the incentives to develop them among its workforce.

The difficulty begins with recruitment—or more precisely with the lack of recruitment. Because State has so many talented people applying for its ranks, it accepts their abilities as validation without screening for the skills it has determined the current force lacks. Once in the door in the Foreign Service and civil service, people tend to remain for an entire career. With an attrition rate of only 4 percent across a professional lifetime and a closed personnel system, the people who are hired are the people who will reach the top ranks. And within the system, they receive almost no education other than for language. All three of these elements—hiring by general talent rather than specific skill, the closed personnel system, and lack of professional development—probably need to be changed. At least one of them does.

Not only should the Foreign Service change the examination and interview process to highlight specific proficiencies the current corps of diplomats lacks, it should actively recruit people from fields where those proficiencies are in use. Painful as it will be for the Foreign Service, both its union and its job security should be called into question, because neither serves the overriding national interest of an adaptive cadre of diplomats. Secretary Rumsfeld attempted a similar change for civilians working in the Defense Department, succeeded for a time, and was then hemmed in by Congress. But attitudes are changing about public sector unions. And nowhere is the argument weaker for unionized labor than in front-line national security jobs.

The 16:1 applicant-to-acceptance ratio for Foreign Service hiring suggests the market-clearing pay rate is significantly lower than what is on offer. Rather than reduce pay to bring price and availability into balance, it would benefit State more to introduce flexibility into its hiring tables. Instead of tenure, the personnel model should shift to limited contracts of perhaps five years, renewable successively for the duration of a career if the diplomat's skills and willingness to undertake assignments of priority for the department continue to align with the State Department's needs. This gives diplomats incentives to expand their skills and accept hardship and war zone assignments. It also will discourage people who are seeking job security as a personal priority, bringing in a more risk-tolerant and entrepreneurial type that matches more closely the "cargo pants" rather than "pin stripes" mentality that current American diplomacy requires.

State will argue that so limber a system will create turmoil, with unexpected shortfalls in personnel that cannot be compensated for. True, a diplomatic corps without tenure would make personnel management more demanding, causing State to monitor more closely what the service's needs are and developing targeted incentives to recruit and retain the necessary people. But that is not an unmanageable circumstance. American businesses and even the American military have personnel tracking and pay systems that target scarce skills for retention. A more turbulent personnel system would also produce a better alignment of skills and pay with requirements, as the messy capitalism of the market demonstrates so well.

State will also argue that the military does not permit lateral moves into its leadership; leaders are grown, acquiring essential skills as their responsibilities increase. But that is not entirely true. First, there are citizen soldiers: our National Guard and Reserve. These part-time military officers and enlisted members have other occupations and are called up for service when the nation is in need. Typically, call-ups are in response to natural disasters or major wars, but one little-noticed change after 9/11 has been the inclusion of National Guard and Reserve units in the rotation of units for Iraq and Afghanistan. The demands of the wars neces-sitated routine use of National Guard units because the size of the Army and Marine Corps was inadequate to the demand for forces. To their great credit, our citizen soldiers have accepted this unexpected responsibility and performed admirably.

Moreover, the resistance to lateral moves into the diplomatic corps ignores an essential difference between military force and diplomacy, which is the government's monopoly on its use. There is no diplomatic equivalent to combat in which a leader's judg-ment is tested and lives hang in the balance. It is substantially more difficult to gain the expertise of military skill in non-military occupations, whereas the crucial skills of successful diplomacy are in more general use. One may become an armchair strategist by studying warfare, but one only becomes a combat leader by leading in combat. On the other hand, corporate leaders, legis-lators, labor arbitrators, and mothers adjudicating quarrelsome children all have some elements of the skills that make for suc-cessful diplomats. Warfare is a more demanding operational field than diplomacy—and than most other human endeavors. That we grow our leaders in the military does not argue against bring-ing in leaders for other skilled professions.

The final refutation to resistance by State to more flexible hir-ing at all levels is that State itself does not invest in training and grooming its professionals beyond their on-the-job training. If professional growth within the Foreign Service and civil service were essential to successful service in higher grades, wouldn't you think State would make that education and training a priority? It does not.

In addition to changing who is hired initially, State should do much more to foster mid-career opportunities in key skill areas. Such an approach would be especially valuable in areas like infor-mation technology and business management. *The Embassy of the Future* concludes ". . . the advances the State Department needs to make are already normal practice outside government."[12] There is a strong bias against mid-career hiring, even though the department cannot claim that it invests in skill development that would make diplomats functionally more capable than lateral transfers from the private sector.

The department needs to usher in a different approach to personnel management soon, because it faces an actuarial problem. State has hired a bow wave of junior diplomats in the past decade, and unless the personnel system is made more flexible, we will in a decade or so have a surfeit of senior diplomats, many more than are needed for senior postings. Currently, half of all diplomats have less than ten years of experience, while more than a quarter have less than five years experience.

Now we are struggling with the problems of too few mentors to provide the counsel on which State's model of professional development depends. In another decade we will be struggling with a top-heavy diplomatic corps frustrated at lack of opportunity for promotion. Even worse would be a department that has inflated positions previously held by lower-grade diplomats. In the Quadrennial Diplomacy and Development Review one can already detect the creation of more senior positions into which a diplomatic corps growing in seniority will be able to have stature—we will be awash in proconsuls. Greater mixing of seniority and functional expertise in consular assignments will also help manage the actuarial problem of too many senior diplomats that is currently on the horizon by blurring somewhat the lines of stature.

One solution to this problem would be to expand the base of the pyramid and narrow its peak, so that entry-level positions are more numerous and the department can afford to be much pickier about the people it advances to senior positions. The current 95 percent tenure rate allows the department almost no latitude in selection—those who come in the door will be advanced to career

employment. Whether they are exceptionally intelligent, diplomatic, and hard-working weighs too little in advancement. Surely
this is inadequate for the world's leading power in determining
the composition of its diplomatic corps.

Another possible solution would be encouraging much more
fluid entry and exit. The Coordinator for Reconstruction and
Stabilization has spent years developing a roster of government
employees who could be called up for deployment. Why not
expand that program beyond government employees to American
society? State does very little to tap into the wealth of diversity
our country contains. Los Angeles is the second largest Iranian
city in the world, ahead of any but Tehran, and the United States
also has large concentrations of other nationalities and languages.
We could build a cadre of Farsi and Hmong and Japanese and
other linguistically proficient Americans, develop pay scales for
participation and deployment just as the National Guard does,
process security clearances, and have a motivated community of
experts on countries and languages in reserve.

State has begun to tentatively explore alternative hiring practices to address its shortfalls. The QDDR suggests expanding the
use of fellowships to bring in technical experts; creating limited
contracts for temporary service; and allowing civil servants,
USAID employees, and foreign national employees greater ability to track into the Senior Foreign Service. Welcome as these
methods are, they affect only at the margin the magnitude of the
problem State is facing. Its current personnel system serves its
needs poorly and is now poised to collapse under the eventual
top-heavy weight of recent hiring.

State should radically reconsider its approach to personnel
management, facilitating careers of five or ten years rather than
a whole professional life; encouraging skilled people to participate in advancing our nation's interests by undertaking a stint
as a diplomat at some point in their careers; and limbering up

the system to reduce incentives for longevity for some employees while increasing them for people with the kinds of skills that will make the culture of the Foreign Service more modern and pliable.

Professional Development

The problems associated with a near complete promotion rate in the Foreign Service are compounded by the lack of education within it. With the exception of a management course instituted by Secretary Powell, our diplomats are provided no training, other than in languages, and no education at all in their professional development. State's model is premised on the assumption that people coming into the Foreign Service have all the education necessary, and requisite training can be provided on the job. But this is clearly not true; State's own descriptions of shortcomings in essential skills refute it.

In 2003, Powell went to Congress asking for an additional 1,000 Foreign Service officers to allow a "training float"—enough personnel that even highly sought-after staffers could build educational opportunities into their career development. Congress provided the positions, but the people were assigned to new priorities, like staffing up the embassy in Baghdad. Secretary Rice eventually persuaded Congress to add staff for "transformational diplomacy" and those, too, were diverted. Secretary Clinton's 3.0 program envisions further staff expansion, yet allots no opportunities for greater intellectual investment in the Foreign Service. Congress keeps providing the resources for educational opportunities, and the institution keeps identifying higher priorities to soak up the additional resources.

So it is discouraging to hear State yet again claim in the Quadrennial Diplomacy and Development Review that "to ensure that the long-term objective of training is not compromised by short-term staffing needs, we must continue to build the personnel ranks at State and USAID."[13] Having been thrice given the personnel to create an education program, State now informs us more personnel will be needed; and it has not yet determined how many people it might require or what the program of providing that education would encompass.

A serious professional development program for diplomats should begin with a thorough review of the work undertaken by diplomats at every level. What are the skills needed from the outset of the profession? At what career thresholds do different skills become important? Are there particular experiences before or after which diplomats would particularly benefit from a pause from activity for reflection and learning?

Once that information is determined, a program can be built that explicitly identifies skills and builds intellectual capital for their successful performance. The program would benefit from being communal as well as individual; that is, from having diplomats engaged in learning physically in the same place. A residency requirement would build on State's tradition of mentoring and would strengthen peer-to-peer bonds as diplomats share experiences and learn from each other.

The Foreign Service Institute in northern Virginia would be one place to conduct this education. It would be the easiest place, as not requiring construction of a campus or additional moves for diplomatic families. It would, however, not be the optimal location. Being in striking distance of Washington, D.C., will tempt both students and faculty to be engaged only part-time (as they are now in the Institute's courses). A better model would be creating the equivalent of the military services' staff colleges, a site where diplomats and their families would be posted for a year to immerse themselves in learning, respite, and collegiality. Locating the college in Seattle or California or Colorado would give a different feel to the campus, taking diplomats out of the policy corridors and plunking them down in the innovation corridor of the West. This would reacquaint them with a part of the country from which their careers keep them distant, stitching them more into the fabric of America in all its diversity.

In the military, educational opportunities are staged before and after command: before to prepare the commander, and after to decompress and reflect on the experience. State should at a minimum build education into a diplomat's career before that person becomes a deputy chief of mission (just below ambassador). Due to the large numbers of political appointees in ambassadorships, capable DCMs are essential to the effective functioning of embassies. Another earlier career threshold where a break for education would naturally fall would be prior to a diplomat having responsibility for supervising an office or section of an embassy. Building extensive education and training into a diplomat's profession at these functional thresholds of roughly the ten- and twenty-year marks would also align the opportunities to people who choose, and are selected for, service in higher grades.

Developing a curriculum that prepares diplomats along State's timelines and responsibilities will be a relatively easy task. In fact, diplomats are already good at this, as the voluntary coursework associated with the Foreign Service Institute and the diplomatic component of the National Defense University show. What is lacking is not coursework of intellectual interest, but a structured curriculum that would provide a standardized floor of expertise in the diplomatic corps.

The Foreign Service has an enormous number of intelligent, educated people who would excel at developing an educational system for their department. They hesitate to sketch that horizon line, though, because the Foreign Service is culturally disinclined to value it and because they literally can no longer imagine having the financial and leadership support to undertake and institutionalize a rigorous education within the Foreign Service.

Given the cultural resistance to education in the Foreign Service, external impetus will likely be necessary to induce its adoption. Again the military provides a useful parallel: the Goldwater-Nichols defense reforms of 1985 had to impose greater cooperation between the services and require joint service before the military began to value it. State's track record on education justifies similar legislative intrusion to force the culture to adopt practices that will improve it. Congressional oversight committees should develop a rubric for State reform that would fund a diplomatic staff college, establish a dedicated training float, and require completion of education at both the office director and deputy chief of mission levels to qualify diplomats for promotion and assignment to those positions. Congress should also provide a reasonable grace period of perhaps eight years for development and adoption of the standards. Beyond that, individual exemptions notified to the Congress should be required.

A diplomatic education and training program needs a means of testing proficiency and rewarding it.[14] Language already has this; diplomats are tested and remuneration tied to retaining their skills. In no other area are our Foreign Service workers required to certify their skills or given incentives to acquire and maintain proficiency. The Embassy of the Future project suggests the Foreign Service establish performance standards and reward competency in these areas in which it lacks expertise: interagency training, leadership, technology fluency, security skills, hardship post training, and presence post training. (The last two are new types of embassy platforms with a lesser suite of support than other posts and therefore require additional proficiencies by diplomats assigned to them.)

Diplomats should not alone be given responsibility for identifying and assigning reward, lest the system trend too much toward what the institution already values: (1) representing the United States in multilateral organizations and to governments and (2) reporting on activity. Secretary Rice looked into the department's reward system and found that "State gave out thirty awards for political reporting, none for civil-military cooperation, none for deploying to the wars."[15]

Outside evaluators from other government agencies, the National Security Council, Congress, think tanks, innovation industries, academia, and the business world should also be given responsibility for helping State to develop a broader view of its requisite tasks. Technology, economics, and business perspectives in particular are important and are lacking in State's construct of its mission, its tasks, and the means of accomplishing them.

Compensating for that deficiency in State's culture and personnel will require a significant push through management attention, education, and training.

We do a disservice to our diplomats by allowing the State Department to continue shunting off the responsibility of providing them with the education and training they need to be successful. The institution settles for taking slots in military colleges rather than developing staff colleges and a National Diplomatic University to compete with the National War College. The institution simply does not value education even though it identifies shortcomings in the proficiencies of its personnel. As one senior diplomat derisively put it, "They think anybody can do this work."

There is a corpus of knowledge American diplomats should master, identifiable even to the untrained eye: understanding of the major diplomatic achievements and disasters in our country's history; evaluating the statesmanship of historically significant secretaries, ambassadors, and envoys; economic trends that strengthened or weakened countries in the international order; the effect various treaties have had on economic livelihood and strategic stability; instances of drastic change precipitated by technological innovation; the effect of immigration on labor markets and national power.

We deserve diplomats with informed views of whether Benjamin Franklin's, Thomas Jefferson's, or John Adams's tactics were better suited to persuading the French government to provide material assistance and military forces during the American revolution. We deserve diplomats who study the international economic consequences of our domestic Smoot-Hawley tariffs in 1930 and trends in international investment in the decade preceding World War I and have thought about whether patterns of trade and investment can lead to wars. We deserve diplomats who know the effect a woman's educational level has on subsequent childhood mortality and poverty. We deserve diplomats who not only can use social media but are innovators themselves, bringing new technologies into the Foreign Service and finding applications that advance our diplomatic efforts. We deserve diplomats who are involved in nongovernmental organizations, private foundations, businesses, universities, religious groups, and city councils across America whose vibrancy and entrepreneurialism they bring into their diplomatic work.

Our diplomats deserve things, too. They deserve to have us respect their professionalism enough to invest in expanding and refining their expertise and to give them opportunities that will make them both better diplomats and more attractive hires in private industry when they leave public service. They deserve us to think about their professional trajectories in ways that set them up to be successful by giving them the skills they will need before they step into broader responsibilities. As The Embassy of the Future report concludes, "the nature of the job requires not only highly talented individuals, but also individuals who are well prepared to undertake these significant and extremely varied responsibilities."[16]

Education should not be a luxury or a prerequisite for American diplomats; it should be integral to their professional lives in a way that enables their professional success. Congress can help by legislating educational standards prior to promotion, as the Goldwater-Nichols reforms did for the military. State should not be permitted to hold off committing to education programs until it has the optimal number of people and resources; it should be required to develop and execute a professional education system with the personnel it has now and be rewarded with resources when it demonstrates that it is taking the mandate seriously.

Risky Business

Another area ripe for reassessment involves the threats to which diplomats are exposed. The risk to embassies and to diplomatic personnel has increased in the past fifteen years. In response, Congress legislated standards for protection of physical infrastructure. While well-intentioned, the standards have turned our embassies into fortresses that are an impediment to carrying out the functions for which we post diplomats abroad. The difficulties of coming to us are sending us to them, resulting in a more secure embassy building but a more exposed diplomatic corps.

Moreover, the work that needs doing for U.S. missions abroad is pushing diplomats more and more outside embassy walls. Our diplomats cannot participate in local councils or attend protest rallies or meet with jailed dissidents or engage community leaders outside capital cities from within our embassies. The work of engaging foreign governments can be done from Washington; the work of engaging foreign societies must be done in their countries and at their activities.

We take for granted that our military operates in harm's way. Increasingly, our diplomats do, too. Until recently, efforts have focused on how to keep them safer. It is time for us and them to accept that the work they do for our country is inherently dangerous. Instead of focusing solely on their safety, we must balance the risks they run with the value their professional activity brings to our national interest.

This different frame of reference means allowing our diplomats to accept greater risk in the performance of their duties, giving them the means of operating securely and independently, rewarding those who take risks to advance our interests, developing means of evaluating their choices as sensible or unduly risky, and protecting them from condemnation when they make sound judgment calls that turn out badly. It means counter-threat training courses should be expanded at a minimum to all State Department personnel posted to critical and high-threat missions, and probably to all diplomats serving abroad.[17] And it means honoring as heroes those diplomats who sacrifice their lives for the good of our country.

Just as the communications revolution has shifted decision-making down ranks in the military—we fight with strategic corporals and captains now, their choices affecting the course of the war—it is also shifting decision-making down ranks in diplomacy. The choices of junior diplomats in consular activities have major repercussions when it no longer takes the resources of a great power to do great damage. One visa can make the difference in a successful terrorist attack. One desk officer's comments to graduate students can provoke a major diplomatic incident.[18] The model based on ambassadors and assistant secretaries controlling the message no longer works; instead of controlling activity, the department needs to command it by educating and empowering the strategic captains of our diplomacy.

As we begin to think of our diplomats as action heroes rather than cosseted observers, the culture of American diplomacy will change. In fact, the wars in Iraq and Afghanistan have already begun to do that. There is now much more interest in the experience of diplomats who served in Vietnam during the war because their intrepidity is an example to the diplomats undertaking similar counter-insurgency diplomacy today in Iraq and Afghanistan. Confluence with military culture is coming back into fashion because it has produced the best results. The new breed of expeditionary diplomats who specialize in diplomacy amid conflict have the potential to revolutionize how State sees itself, if they are nurtured and allowed opportunities to lead. They have a way to go before they are truly the peers of their military counterparts, but it is at last plausible because of the ways they are adapting to new challenges and providing a model of adaptability to the rest of the department.

The cultural shift from a reporting agency to an activist one will necessitate numerous changes in the mundane details of assignments for diplomats. According to Secretary Rice, ". . . we had problems getting State into the fight, not because people weren't willing, but because State didn't have the right structures to support them."[19] Families of diplomats assigned to war zones were required to be in the United States rather than living in safe nearby countries that facilitated visits. Embassy personnel had to accept subordination to military chains of command in war zones. State has only recently introduced a program that restricts bidding for the most attractive posts to those diplomats who have served recently in hardship posts.[20] Many more such levers will need to be found and used to reshape the Foreign Service such that its most rewarded diplomats are those doing the work of greatest importance to the country.

In addition to physical risk-taking, another element of risk-taking State needs to free up for greater initiative is in policy development and execution. The military makes a distinction between command and control, where command is the setting of objectives and resources and control is the staff function of carrying out the responsibilities. The common complaint among diplomats is too much control from Washington—"the seven-thousand-mile screwdriver," to use the term in vogue from Embassy Baghdad after the Iraq war—and there is reason for their complaint. Technology is enabling a more dispersed concept of operations for American diplomats, if only Washington would give them the latitude to carry out foreign policy that way.

The Embassy of the Future recommends a model "that is substantially 'optimized for the edges'—that is, one in which diplomats have the ability and authority to operate independently at the local level, under broad strategic guidance."[21] A better-educated and -trained cadre of diplomats and higher risk tolerance would increase confidence in Washington that embassies would not need the level of oversight currently practiced, as would a Foreign Service culture less supercilious toward elected and appointed officials. Shifting initiative from Washington to diplomatic posts does occur, especially under ambassadors with strong Washington relationships and willingness to take risks, but bureaucratic processes in the department continue to constrain our diplomats from capitalizing on their presence within countries to maximum effect.

Reconsider Universality

It is taken for granted that the United States must have an embassy in every country in the world. The assumption drives spending and staffing requirements for the Department of State. Traditionally, diplomatic representation in every country was necessitated by diplomatic reciprocity and the need to conduct affairs of state. While reciprocity is sometimes portrayed as an exchange of hostages (brother of the king sent to show you wouldn't risk his life by acting against the country in which he was stationed), its real purpose was to bestow diplomatic recognition.

Long past is the necessity of demonstrating our international importance; in fact, the pendulum has swung so far in the other direction that Washington, D.C., is the global diplomatic center of gravity. Although not something we should do, we probably could even get away with conducting our diplomatic business wholly from Washington.

But the transportation and communications revolutions have dramatically reduced the need for permanently stationed personnel in every country. The days are thankfully gone when getting to a capital was a lengthy, onerous, and often dangerous undertaking. More travel by more private citizens requires consular support but also provides information that once might have been the provenance of official representatives. Reliable, affordable, and accessible communications connections allow crucial work to be performed from outside the country.

Diplomats inside a country can be a liability as well as a benefit. The Obama administration claimed it wanted to take action against Libyan dictator Muammar Gaddafi during the popular uprising there, but was constrained by perceived risk to American diplomats still in country.[22] While President Obama injudiciously encouraged hostile governments to consider American diplomats as hostages, those nations surely did not require his attention to that issue to have thought of it themselves.

In some cases, even political revolutions, like the dissolution of internal boundaries in the countries of the European Union's Schengen treaty, call into question the need for individual embassies. Proximity of the seats of government in Belgium, the Netherlands, and Luxembourg, for example, and the amount of formerly state business they have transferred to the European Union might suggest a circuit-rider approach of non-continuous representation for diplomatic relations in those capitals.

Being present of course has advantages, especially in crises. An ambassador reporting on public demonstrations in an authoritarian country, assessing the stability of the government, and working with local forces to protect and advance our interests is a supremely valuable source of trusted information and conduit of activity for our government. Countries can close their borders to arrivals, making it impossible for our government to bear witness to events and work with local forces. But these are arguments for having representation in most countries, not necessarily all countries, and for weighting the need for representation by additional factors.

Some of the other factors the United States might consider in shifting from universal representation would be demand, accessibility, and security. Demand is an obvious criterion, involving not only how much business an embassy does but also the importance of having those functions undertaken on site. Embassies that provide routine access to government officials in countries whose choices are important to America, process thousands of visas, conduct high-level trade negotiations, or report from within the countries of repressive governments that constrain the activities of journalists and civil society organizations have the most urgent needs for physical representation.

Even here, though, many embassy functions that used to need doing overseas can now be undertaken remotely. Visa processing is trending toward consolidation in U.S. locations where search tools and interagency intelligence databases are accessible. Interviews are even conducted remotely by video now, with no apparent reduction in quality of understanding by U.S. consular officials.

Accessibility is perhaps the most difficult factor to assess. Where there is little access to communications that allow foreigners to tap into U.S. government channels remotely, or where movement within their countries is restricted by poor infrastructure, danger, or convention (restrictions on female travel, for instance), there is greater need for U.S. diplomats to be present and available. Having embassies everywhere probably does reduce the stigma associated with reporting by foreign nationals.

As an example, the father of Umar Abdulmutallab visited the U.S. embassy in Nigeria to report on his son's radicalization and location. It is obviously in American interests to have representation that encourages the trust to provide such information to U.S. authorities.

Concern for, and the cost of, protecting American embassies has dramatically increased after attacks on them and might also suggest reconsidering the assumption of embassies in every country. As literal bastions of American power, they are iconic terrorist targets. Congress now requires by law standards of defensibility that have driven many embassies out of central locations and into veritable fortresses complete with living compounds. These security standards work at conflicting purposes with our interests in showcasing the openness of American society and encouraging wide and diverse interaction with individuals and groups in the countries where our embassies operate.

State has experimented in recent years with varying types of representation: single-diplomat outposts, virtual embassies that exist only on the internet, "American corners" staffed by foreign nationals that provide internet access to U.S. government sites, and traveling teams of American diplomats to expand the reach of services beyond embassies and consulates. This kind of creativity should be further encouraged to expand the scope of inquiry into whether standing diplomatic representation is needed in every country in the world at all times.

Chronic Underfunding

Former Secretary of Defense Robert Gates is the most ardent advocate for increasing spending on the non-military levers of American power. No one has made the case more often or more persuasively than he that we have "a need for a dramatic increase

in spending on the civilian instruments of national security—
diplomacy, strategic communications, foreign assistance, civic
action, and economic reconstruction and development."[23] Gates
is closely followed in this by former Chairman of the Joint Chiefs
of Staff Admiral Michael Mullen, who served as the president's
senior military advisor. Their advocacy was instrumental in persuading Congress to increase spending on diplomacy and development. They have also, in a very minor way, put their money
where their mouths are, agreeing to a $100 million contingency
operations fund, allowing State to draw on DOD funds.[24]

It is, however, cause for continued concern that State cannot more forcefully make the case for itself, especially since the
funding levels State aspires to are pathetically little compared
to the money Congress has long been at ease spending on the
military. What is striking in the literature on improving the State
Department is how minor are the requests anticipated to revolutionize the practice of diplomacy and create the capacity for
whole-of-government operations.

Proposals for improvement in diplomatic performance include
things like establishing a cadre of human resources professionals,
requiring seven to ten additional medium-ranking government
employees, at a total annual cost of between $1.33 million and
$1.9 million.[25] Or this, from Secretary Clinton's Diplomacy 3.0:
"Require that all officers going into positions where they will
oversee new employees take a short course—perhaps through
distance learning—on supervising and mentoring new employees." Or this, from the Quadrennial Diplomacy and Development
Review: "State and USAID will set high standards for the integration of up-to-date empirical evidence into the development of
strategies and programs. Operationally, this means: Senior officials will communicate."[26] What is so discouraging about reform-
ing the Department of State is that so many obvious improvements
are described but not undertaken. These are not Einstein's three

unsolved equations; they are basic management problems ame-nable to analysis and leadership.

The proposals for improvement from State officials are all so modest and marginal that one begins to wonder whether they actu-ally understand what it would take to make themselves a vibrant, successful organization. There is no root-and-branch reconsidera-tion of the business model, no reconceptualization of the mission and organization, no engagement with futurists to imagine the discontinuities that could fracture our current approach, no busi-ness board to review the department's plans for soundness and affordability, no red team to challenge cost estimates or force a competition of ideas, no enforcement of the secretary's authority over the bureaucracy to implement the president's priorities.

In no current proposal for improving the State Department does the sticker price for perfecting American diplomacy come to more than 135 percent of current spending. Not even the wildest-eyed dreamer of a diplomatically dominated U.S. national security establishment would increase the budget by more than a third over current spending. In a twisted way, this lack of ambition shows how much State has reduced its expectations for achievement—it doesn't even know how to gold-plate budget requests or imagine innovative and expensive approaches to its profession or tools to enable its success.

If State is to solve the chronic underfunding that so distorts the institution and its culture, it must learn to make its case persua-sively to the Congress. That begins with developing a program-matic culture in the department that collects and analyzes data, creating metrics by which it can judge performance and argue for resources, and utilizing those metrics to draft a long-term budget so that Congress can see where annual spending aggregates into capabilities.

The budget process within State does not align spending to the secretary's priorities. When asked by Secretary Rice to show the figures for the president's top diplomatic priority of democracy promotion, the department's budget analysts could not produce them, nor did they think they ought to have to.[27]

The Quadrennial Diplomacy and Development Review says the right things about "establishing consistent indicators," "investing in development or strengthening of key data sources," "reviewing existing evaluation," and "establishing a strategic planning and budgeting process, including multi-year budgeting."[28] Yet it consigns them to future development; with two years' work on the QDDR, the metrics should already be in place.

The Defense Department annually puts out a Future Years Defense Program, which begins with the current year's spending request and lays out a rolling five-year budget. This FYDP allows Congress to see where the department is headed, to determine whether it supports the direction, and to highlight any increases in cost or divergences in spending from the levels and priorities to which Congress has agreed. In theory, the Future Years Defense Program is the budgetary translation of the Quadrennial Defense Review; when those two planning documents fail to connect, Congress rightly questions the secretary on their divergence. Through the FYDP, Congress is given the information necessary to grade the Pentagon's performance, the means to hold it accountable for its choices, and the strategic plan to garner congressional support. That State has not seen fit to provide Congress with a projection that connects present spending to agreed longer-term outcomes is a huge bureaucratic shortfall and a central reason Congress distrusts State Department spending figures.

What is urgently needed in the Department of State right now is an analytic basis for determining requirements and a business plan for delivering the resources. Mostly, what State considers assessment comes down to saying that if it is given more money, it can do its job better. State's advocates believe it as an article of faith, whereas its critics use it as proof that State cannot be entrusted with more money. The main message out of State's first ever Quadrennial Diplomacy and Development Review is that diplomacy is cost-effective national security. It does not provide the basis for making that judgment, however, and doing so will be essential in building confidence that monies allocated to the Department of State are the best marginal investment of scarce national security dollars.

What Right Looks Like

None of the proposals advocated here are rocket science. Focusing more tightly on consular activity as the department's raison d'être, limbering up the personnel system, providing professional education, encouraging greater risk tolerance in performance of duty, reconsidering where representation needs to be physically located, and establishing a stable basis for long-term funding are all basic elements of good management. They are things routinely practiced in successful businesses and organizations.

Such business practices are not routinely undertaken in the management of the U.S. Department of State. In part, this is because secretaries of state tend not to undertake internal management initiatives. They run the department from their seventh-floor suite of offices through their political appointees and focus on foreign policies rather than investing in improving the performance of the department as a whole. This is to some extent understandable, given how resistant the culture of the Foreign Service is to initiative from political direction.

But the dearth of solid management in State also occurs because we don't demand it of the leadership in the State Department. The president typically appoints secretaries of defense who are proven managers of business operations; after all, they are being brought in to run a $583 billion organization whose business directly affects the sovereignty and wealth of the country. Secretaries of state tend to be political luminaries or foreign policy experts, many of whom have no prior managerial experience and virtually none of whom have had experience in the private sector. We expect less of secretaries of state, with their smaller budgets and fuzzier determination of success or failure.

We should not do that, however. We ought to care enough about the success of our diplomatic endeavors that we demand a leadership capable of both external initiative and sound management of the business. Indeed, unless we are willing to see fundamentally civilian diplomatic tasks continue to migrate to (and burden) our military, we need to get serious about running the State Department as a successful business.

A business-like approach to diplomacy begins with putting systems in place that capitalize on the strengths of the organization and that do not depend on excellence for their basic fulfillment. The American Academy of Diplomacy says it best:

> A more systematic approach to building and sustaining the skills and knowledge of diplomacy will be needed to enable America's diplomats effectively to carry their share of the international affairs burden.[29]

Instead of expecting individual excellence to define the system, we should be working to provide bureaucratic means that facilitate success by average performers. In short, we need to take an entrepreneurial approach to raising the mean performance of the organization.

Diplomacy is war by other means, and we must take its practice as seriously as we take the practice of warfare. We need to value our diplomacy and our diplomats enough to create a culture of leadership within the department, and from it derive the management tools to strengthen performance. Only by doing so can we realize the goal of making the Department of State a genuine partner and peer to the Department of Defense. For State to truly lead through civilian power, it must have the means to attract support. Diplomacy will not become the integrator of agencies and effort until the State Department demonstrates the ability to lead because it has essential tools. The most powerful of those tools is our diplomats. We must believe in them, invest in them, and create the conditions in which they are going to be successful.

CHAPTER 6

Program

The Department of State is an underperforming institution. It has significant reservoirs of capability but it makes poor use of them; it has needs it cannot find ways to meet. Its institutional reflex is to complain it lacks the resources to create change—most recently demonstrated in the QDDR's insistence that State needs more money and more people in order to support training. Thus State both justifies its current inadequacy and shields itself from reforms that would improve the organization.

What is so discouraging about analyzing the Department of State is how eminently fixable its problems are. Businesses and organizations all over the United States remedy these kinds of problems routinely. Doing so requires management committed to rigorous assessment of the organization's failings, development of a program for change, and consistent attention to that plan's implementation. Currently, the Department of State has none of these three elements.

Ideally, the impetus for creating them should lie within the State Department. And, in theory, State has begun that process with the QDDR. Yet the organization's vision remains wedded to activities that neglect core functions (consular activity and training) and elevate activities and people that replicate the existing priorities.

Making the Department of State better at its job will require either imposition of change from outside or an internal management much more committed to improved performance. External efforts could come in the form of legislative requirements and reporting established by Congress or internal administration guidelines that could be free-standing or attached to budget production.

Much of the reorientation could come from within State itself—indeed, nothing proposed in this book is unattainable by State alone and acting within its current budget parameters. What follows is a brief list of activity to begin a process of informing and administering change that will improve America's diplomacy.

Executive or Legislative Action:

★ Initiate transition to limited contract hiring and away from tenured Foreign Service and civil service

★ Recruit and encourage acquisition of skills in short supply

★ Allow mid-career hires to fill identified skill shortfalls

★ Establish requirement for professional education at the ten-year and twenty-year marks

★ Require completion of education prior to consideration for promotion

★ Penalize State for not tracking staff into professional education and for not developing education and training programs

★ Require metrics for review of staffing and workloads and for number and location of embassies

★ Require annual QDDR implementation reports

★ Require development of a Future Years Diplomatic Program to lengthen State programmatic analyses out to five years

★ Review security requirements for embassies and personnel

Task State to:

★ Focus on consular work as the center of institutional gravity

★ Reward consular service as the essential function of the department

★ Assess essential skill sets, both for whole-of-government functions and for those functions necessarily resident within State/USAID

★ Identify specialized talent pools and recruit from them

★ Develop curricula for professional education and training

★ Establish and staff diplomatic schools

★ Test for achievement of greater specialized expertise

★ Create pilot programs to hire more mid-career experts for limited terms of service

★ Finish the work of the Office of the Coordinator for Reconstruction and Stabilization to develop a program similar to the National Guard for bringing citizen-diplomats into service when the areas of their expertise (language, logistics, etc.) are needed

★ Develop metrics for review of staffing and workloads

★ Collect and analyze significantly more data on policy implementation and cost-effectiveness

★ Develop a five-year rolling budget for congressional review

★ Align strategic planning (the Quadrennial Diplomacy and Development Review) with annual budgets

★ Review personnel policies that inhibit deployments to war zones

★ Align personnel assignments and promotions with department needs (move beyond just filling hardship posts to longer-term career planning)

★ Encourage analytic assessments and policy implementation in personnel policies

★ Provide embassy reporting on implementation of policies under consideration

★ Force the culture to confront the fact that without managerial skills, State will not be the agency of choice to manage whole-of-government activity

CHAPTER 7

Conclusion

This book developed in reaction to the proposition that America's civilian agencies could not be made successful. Carl Schramm's "Expeditionary Economics" framework (described in his article in the May/June 2010 edition of *Foreign Affairs*) takes as a given that members of the economic development community—both diplomats and development professionals—are incapable of understanding the nature of current demands or of crafting successful strategies for achieving their essential contributions to America's war efforts in Iraq and Afghanistan.

I believe that is untrue—or at least should be untrue. Our country should not accept the idea that the organizations tasked with essential functions should be allowed to function badly. Yet the empirical evidence supports the claims in "Expeditionary Economics": our development community has not fostered development and our diplomats are inadequate to the tasks of operating in dangerous and rapidly changing environments to build capacity for governance and capitalize on hard-won military gains.

That it has been true is not an argument for it remaining so, however. There is not an immutable reason that State should

perform less well than does Defense. We make choices as a government that produce success or failure. In the case of the Defense
Department, we choose to fund it liberally, set very high standards for its performance, and populate it with leaders who take
the profession and its professionalism seriously. In the case of the
State Department, we choose to fund it penuriously, set no real
standards for its performance, and populate it with leaders who
do not invest in making the institution or its people successful.
They work around the difficulties of the organization rather than
fixing them.

We could accept the conclusions of "Expeditionary Economics" and make the Defense Department good at the work that the
Department of State and the U.S. Agency for International Development should do. I believe that would be wrong. It would be
wrong to allow the continued atrophy of America's diplomatic
power simply because it is hard work to improve the performance
of a civilian agency that has long tolerated underperformance.
It is hard work to improve the performance of our military, too,
but we make the choice to do that work. We need also to make
the choice to do the hard work of making our State Department a
beacon of excellence in its work.

America needs a State Department that attracts entrepreneurial people and then develops in them the means—and gives them
the support—to effectively promote American values and interests
throughout the world. We need a State Department that makes
possible the projection of American civilian power and capital-
izes on the use of American military force . . . a State Department
that cultivates support by understanding and solving problems,
our own and those of other countries . . . a State Department that
has as its core mission the protection of Americans at home and
abroad and that has built a solid basis of domestic support for its
needs and activities.

Such a State Department is within reach. We know how to do these things—we do them routinely in other organizations. We just haven't bothered to do them in the Department of State. Yet we could; with difficulty and sustained effort, across perhaps ten years, we could grow an American diplomatic corps that is the real peer of our fighting men and women. We owe it to our diplomats to make that effort, and we owe it to the Soldiers, Sailors, Airmen and Marines of our military to take diplomacy as seriously as we take warfare.

NOTES

Chapter One

1. Carl Schramm, "Expeditionary Economics," *Foreign Affairs*, May/June 2010.
2. For my assessment of the problems associated with military responsibility for development, see Kori Schake, "Operationalizing Expeditionary Economics," *Proceedings from the Summit on Entrepreneurship and Expeditionary Economics: Toward A New Approach to Economic Growth Following Conflict or Disaster*, Kauffman Foundation, 2010.

Chapter Two

1. American Academy of Diplomacy and the Henry L. Stimson Center, *A Foreign Affairs Budget for the Future: Fixing the Crisis in Diplomatic Readiness*, October 2008, p. 19, http://www.stimson.org/books-reports /a-foreign-affairs-budget-for-the-future-fixing-the-crisis-in-diplomatic -readiness.
2. The conclusion was reached in two pilot evaluations required by the Office of Personnel Management; State has not undertaken a comprehensive evaluation but did include—and thereby endorse—the OPM conclusion in the *Quadrennial Diplomacy and Development Review* (QDDR), p. 179.
3. Secretary Clinton, *The First Quadrennial Diplomacy and Development Review: Leading Through Civilian Power* (Washington DC: U.S. State Department, December 2010), introduction, p. i.

4. For an assessment of the "civilian surge" and in particular the governance programs, see Josh Boak, "In Afghanistan, U.S. 'civilian surge' falls short in building local government," *Washington Post*, March 8, 2011, http://www.washingtonpost.com/wp-dyn/content/article/2011/03/08/AR2011030805351.html (viewed March 8, 2011).
5. See Secretary Gates' letter dated April 21, 2010, to Senate Budget Chairman Kent Conrad, http://www.state.gov/documents/organization/140886.pdf (viewed March 8, 2010).
6. *A Foreign Affairs Budget for the Future*, p. iv.
7. Department of State, "FY 2011 International Affairs Budget," http://www.state.gov/s/d/rm/c35249.htm (viewed March 8, 2011). Congress did not enact a spending bill for FY2011; numbers given are State's proposed budget.

Chapter Three

1. See, for example, Secretary Clinton's introduction to the QDDR and pages 1, 8, and 29.
2. Condoleezza Rice, interview, August 11, 2011.
3. Gallup has been conducting the poll since 1975, and the military has consistently topped the rankings, most recently by more than 15 percentage points over any other institution. Lydia Saad, "Americans' Confidence in Military Up, Banks Down," Gallup, June 24, 2009, http://www.gallup.com/poll/121214/americans-confidence-military-banks-down.aspx (viewed January 31, 2011).
4. Deputy Secretary Richard Armitage, "Testimony Before the Senate Foreign Relations Committee," March 15, 2001, http://usinfo.org/wf-archive/2001/010315/epf408.htm (viewed September 21, 2011).
5. *A Foreign Affairs Budget for the Future*, p. 13.
6. Lieutenant General Mark Hertling, Deputy Commander, U.S. Army Training and Doctrine Command, interviewed January 31, 2011.
7. Joseph J. Ellis, *First Family: Abigail and John Adams* (New York: Alfred A. Knopf, 2010), p. 76.
8. One metric of the influence of Europeanists in the Foreign Service is the specialty of the Foreign Service officers who have been selected as undersecretary for policy, the most senior and influential job typically afforded a career diplomat. Nearly all of them have come from ambassadorships in European countries.
9. President Dwight D. Eisenhower, quoted in "Memorandum of Discussion at the 285th Meeting of the National Security

Council," May 17, 1956, *Foreign Relations of the United States*, vol. 19, p. 310.

10. Dean Acheson, *Present At the Creation: My Years in the State Department* (New York: W.W. Norton, 1969), p. 39.

11. Ibid., p. 38.

12. Ibid., p. 88.

13. Joseph J. Ellis, *His Excellency: George Washington* (New York: Vintage Books, 2005), p. xii.

14. Office of the United States Trade Representative, "History of the United States Trade Representative," http://www.ustr.gov/about-us/history (viewed January 31, 2011).

15. U.S. Agency for International Development, "USAID History," http://www.usaid.gov/about_usaid/usaidhist.html (viewed January 31, 2011).

16. *A Foreign Affairs Budget for the Future*, p. 61.

17. QDDR, p. 167. Incidentally, State's proposed solution to this shortfall of key capability is to increase science and technology fellowships and re-hire retired Foreign Service Officers.

18. Condoleezza Rice, interview, August 11, 2011.

19. American Academy of Diplomacy, American Foreign Service Association, and the Henry L. Stimson Center. *Forging a 21st-century Diplomatic Service for the United States through Professional Education and Training*, 2011, p. 9.

20. *A Foreign Affairs Budget for the Future*, pg 3.

21. Matt Armstrong, "American Public Diplomacy Wears Combat Boots: Proposed Strategic Communication Management Board to Advise the Secretary of Defense," *MountainRunner*, May 19, 2008, http://mountainrunner.us/2008/05/american_public_diplomacy_wear_1.html (viewed February 1, 2011).

22. The 2005 decision is contained in National Security Presidential Directive 44, December 7, 2005. Assessment of the deficiencies is from *A Foreign Affairs Budget for the Future*, p. 49.

23. *A Foreign Affairs Budget for the Future*, p. 50.

24. Lieutenant General Mike Barbero, Iraq Deputy Commanding General for Advising and Training, Pentagon Briefing, July 18, 2010, http://www.usf-iraq.com/news/press-briefings/pentagon-dod-news-briefing-with-lt-gen-barbero-june-18- (viewed February 1, 2011).

25. Inspector General Stuart Bowen, cited in "U.S. Oversight of Iraq Police Training Firm Faulted," Reuters, January 25, 2010, http://www.reuters.com/article/2010/01/25/us-iraq-usa-report-idUSTRE60O14820100125 (viewed February 1, 2011).

26. In this regard, Secretary Rice pointed out that the Foreign Service board that nominates ambassadors did not consider prior service in conflict zones a relevant criterion, even for postings to Iraq, Afghanistan, and Pakistan. Condoleezza Rice, interview, August 11, 2011.

27. QDDR, p. 54.

28. Fact Sheet, Bureau of Human Resources, Department of State (HR), June 30, 2010. Full-time permanent employees totaled 65,689, including about 7,458 Foreign Service officers, 5,401 Foreign Service specialists, 9,914 members of the civil service, and 42,916 locally employed staff (host-country or third-country nationals employed by U.S. missions abroad).

29. QDDR, p. 164.

30. Ibid., p. 170.

31. Profiles of the 150th, 151st, 152nd, and 153rd A-100 classes provided by the American Foreign Service Association (AFSA), quoted in *Forging a 21st-century Diplomatic Service*, pg. 39.

32. *Forging a 21st-century Diplomatic Service*, pg 58.

33. QDDR Executive Summary, p. 12.

34. QDDR, p. 166.

35. *Forging a 21st-century Diplomatic Service*, p. 25.

36. QDDR, pp. 165–166.

37. U.S. Department of State, "Congressional Budget Justification," vol. 1, Department of State Operations, Fiscal Year 2011, pp. ix and 43.

38. Part of the deficit is attributable to the department's more demanding approach to language competence. The number of language-designated positions has doubled since 2001. The number of positions requiring competence in Arabic has increased fivefold. U.S. Department of State, Bureau of Human Resources, "FY 2010 Personnel Strategy Report," pp. 6–7.

39. General Accounting Office, "State Department: Professional Development of Foreign Service Employees," NSIAD-89-149, July 26, 1989, p. 3.

40. *A Foreign Affairs Budget for the Future*, p. 24.

41. Center for Strategic and International Studies, *The Embassy of the Future*, October 2007, p. 8.

42. Philippe Lussier, quoted in Bob Guldin, "Diplomacy 3.0: A Progress Report," *Foreign Service Journal*, May 2010, p. 25.

43. *A Foreign Affairs Budget for the Future*, p. 21.

44. This is also the conclusion of the report by Kristin Lord and Richard Fontaine, "Managing 21st Century Diplomacy: Lessons from Global Corporations," Center for a New American Security,

December 15, 2010, http://www.cnas.org/node/5436, viewed
September 21, 2011.

45. *Forging a 21st-century Diplomatic Service*, p. 33.

46. *Forging a 21st-century Diplomatic Service*, p. 23.

47. Guldin, "Diplomacy 3.0: A Progress Report," p. 28.

48. Figure based on two pilot evaluations required by the Office of Personnel
Management; State has not undertaken a comprehensive evaluation.
QDDR, p. 179.

49. *A Foreign Affairs Budget for the Future*, p. 19.

50. QDDR, p. 164.

51. Stanford University in 2010 had 32,022 undergraduate applicants and
admitted 2,340, a comparable 7.3 percent acceptance rate. For most
recent Applicant Profile figures at Stanford University, see http://
admission.stanford.edu/basics/selection/profile.html.

52. This contrast was drawn by Ambassador Eric Edelman, interview,
May 2011.

53. QDDR, p. 165.

54. *A Foreign Affairs Budget for the Future*, p. 60.

55. This program goes by the easily satirized name Super-Critical Languages
Program.

56. QDDR, p. 167.

57. "FY-2010 Personnel Strategy Report," p. 8.

58. Ambassador Robert Loftis, interview, February 18, 2011.

59. *A Foreign Affairs Budget for the Future*, p. 3, 10.

60. Ibid., pp. 2, 11–12.

61. *The Embassy of the Future*, p. 5.

62. *Forging a 21st-century Diplomatic Service*, p. 11.

63. Kevin Baron, "Marine Commandant Concluded DADT Repeal May
Risk Lives," *Stars and Stripes*, December 14, 2010, http://www.stripes
.com/news/marine-commandant-concluded-dadt-repeal-may-risk
-lives-1.128737 (viewed February 2, 2011); Ed O'Keefe, "Top Marines
Pledge to 'Step Out Smartly' To Repeal Don't Ask Don't Tell,"
Washington Post, January 31, 2011, http://voices.washingtonpost.com
/federal-eye/2011/01/top_marines_pledge_to_step_out_1.html (viewed
February 2, 2011).

64. Acheson, *Present at the Creation*, p. 157.

65. These are outlined in the Foreign Service Act of 1980 (P.L. 96-465), as
amended, 22 U.S.C. 3901, on the careers.state.gov section of its Web site
and at usaid.gov/careers.

66. *The Embassy of the Future*, Executive Summary, pg. vi.

67. Army Commissioned Officer Career Information, Military Schools. About.com: US Military, http://usmilitary.about.com/library/milinfo /arofficerinfo/blmilschools.htm.

68. *The Embassy of the Future*, p. 20.

69. *Forging a 21st-century Diplomatic Service*, p. 38.

70. "FY-2010 Personnel Strategy Report," p. 5.

71. See, for example, the American Academy of Diplomacy's *Forging a 21st-century Diplomatic Service* and the Stimson Center's *A Foreign Affairs Budget for the Future*, p. 1. The American Academy of Diplomacy report recommends an increase from 11,772 in FY08 to 14,663 in FY13 to eradicate staffing shortfalls and permit professional education similar to that of the military. Table 1.1, *Forging a 21st-century Diplomatic Service*, p. 23.

72. U.S. Department of State, *America's Overseas Presence in the 21st Century*, Report of the Overseas Presence Advisory Council (Washington, DC: Government Printing Office, November 1999).

73. "FY 2010 Personnel Strategy Report"; Government Accountability Office, "Additional Steps Needed to Address Continuing Staffing and Experience Gaps at Hardship Posts," GAO-09-874, September 2009, p. 7.

74. Ambassador Ryan Crocker, "Iraq Needs U.S. Engagement and a Slower Clock," *Washington Post*, August 31, 2010, http://www.washingtonpost .com/wp-dyn/content/article/2010/08/30/AR2010083003773.html (viewed February 3, 2011). This assumption in the Joint Campaign Plan was a major point of contention with the advisory panel for the campaign plan, on which I served in 2009.

75. Anthony Cordesman, "Iraq: A Time to Stay? The U.S. Needs an Exit Strategy, Not Just an Exit," Center for Strategic and International Studies, August 1, 2009, p. 1, http://csis.org/files/publication/090731_Iraq -MoreThanExit.pdf (viewed February 4, 2011).

76. General Raymond Odierno, interviewed in *Prism* (National Defense University, vol. 1, no. 2), p. 144, http://www.ndu.edu/press/lib/images /prism1-2/11_Prism_141-148_Odierno.pdf (viewed February 4, 2011).

77. U.S. Congress, Senate Foreign Relations Committee, "Iraq: The Transition from a Military Mission to a Civilian-Led Effort," February 2011, p. 1.

78. Deputy Secretary of State Thomas Nidal, cited in Senate Foreign Relations Committee, "Iraq: The Transition from a Military Mission to a Civilian-Led Effort," p. 16, footnote 20.

79. "Iraq: Transition from a Military to a Civilian-Led Effort," p. 7.

80. Ibid., p. 9.

81. Commission on Wartime Contracting in Iraq and Afghanistan, Special Report 3, July 12, 2010: "Better planning for Defense-to-State

transition in Iraq needed to avoid mistakes and waste," http://www
.wartimecontracting.gov/index.php/reports.

82. "Iraq: The Transition from a Military Mission to a Civilian-Led Effort,"
pg. 11.

83. Cordesman, "Iraq: A Time to Stay?" p. 6.

84. Undersecretary of State Patrick Kennedy, April 7, 2010, letter
to Undersecretary of Defense Ashton Carter, excerpted in "Iraq: The
Transition from a Military Mission to a Civilian-Led Effort," p. 8.

85. QDDR, pp. 200–201.

86. Major General Robert Caslen, quoted in Josh Rogin, "U.S. Embassy in
Baghdad Has Plans to Double in Size," *Foreign Policy*, January 7, 2010,
http://thecable.foreignpolicy.com/posts/2010/01/07/us_embassy_in_
baghdad_has_plans_to_double_in_size (viewed February 3, 2011). The
report, "Iraq: The Transition from a Military Mission to a Civilian-Led
Effort," p. 9, confirms that cost was the determiner of the number of
civilian sites.

87. "Iraq: The Transition from a Military Mission to a Civilian-Led
Effort," p. 2.

88. Ibid. The report also notes that branch offices would have an even lower
tooth-to-tail ratio, with 600 security and support staff to only thirty diplomats, p. 2.

89. "Iraq: The Transition from a Military Mission to a Civilian-Led
Effort," p. 3.

90. Government Accountability Office, "Securing and Stabilizing Iraq: An
Assessment of the Joint Campaign Plan," GAO-10-584R, April 22, 2010,
http://www.gao.gov/products/GAO-10-584R (viewed February 3, 2011).

91. John T. Bennett, "Senators Fear Deficit Focus Will Be Roadblock to
Approval of Iraq Funds," *The Hill*, February 4, 2011, http://thehill.com
/news-by-subject/defense-homeland-security/141997-senators-fear-deficit
-will-be-roadblock-to-approval-of-iraq-funds (viewed February 4, 2011).

92. *Forging a 21st-century Diplomatic Service*, p. 21.

Chapter Four

1. QDDR, pp. 4–5.

2. QDDR Executive Summary, pp.1, 8; QDDR, pp. 29, 37, 86, 1.

3. Anthony Cordesman, "The Quadrennial Diplomacy and Development
Review: Concepts Are Not Enough," Center for Strategic and
International Studies, December 2010, http://csis.org/publication
/quadrennial-diplomacy-and-development-review-qddr.

4. At the time of the 1886 law, six secretaries of state had gone on to
   the presidency: Thomas Jefferson, James Madison, James Monroe,
   John Quincy Adams, Martin van Buren, and James Buchanan (who
   ended his tenure at State in 1849).
5. Condoleezza Rice, interview, August 11, 2011.
6. Department of State, "FY2012 State and USAID–Overseas Contingency
   Operations," February 14, 2011, http://www.state.gov/s/d/rm/rls
   /fs/2011/156555.htm (viewed March 8, 2011).
7. Report of the DOD Inspector General in Iraq, cited in Walter Pincus,
   "Iraqi Security Forces Facing Serious Problems, U.S. Oversight Official
   Reports," *Washington Post*, January 30, 2011, p. 7.
8. QDDR, p. 6.
9. In the instance of Eisenhower's comment, he was cautioning the
   Kennedy administration's Pentagon civilians about their elaborate plans
   for the Berlin Crisis—and, in fact, while they developed more than a
   hundred specific contingency plans, not one of them envisioned East
   Germany infringing on no Western freedom of movement but building
   a barrier inside its own territory to prevent its population from fleeing.
10. QDDR, p. 6.
11. QDDR, p. 74.
12. QDDR, p. 76.
13. QDDR, p. 88.
14. QDDR, p. 100.
15. QDDR, p. 88.
16. QDDR, p. 87.
17. QDDR, p. 96.
18. QDDR, p. 116.
19. QDDR, p. 37.
20. QDDR, p. 13.
21. QDDR, p. 18.
22. QDDR, p. 16.
23. QDDR Executive Summary, p. 14.
24. QDDR Executive Summary, p 7.
25. QDDR Fact Sheet, http://www.state.gov/documents/organization
    /153109.pdf.
26. QDDR, p. 45.
27. QDDR, p. 55.
28. QDDR Executive Summary, p 5.
29. QDDR, p. 29.
30. This is a recommendation also made in the *Embassy of the Future* report
    and many other commissions of former diplomats; it is never endorsed by
    the other agencies affected. *The Embassy of the Future*, p. 49.

31. Colonel Michael Meese, interview, September 6, 2011.
32. QDDR, p. 30.
33. QDDR, pp. 7–8.
34. QDDR, p. 9.
35. QDDR, p. 123.
36. QDDR, p. 122.
37. Colonel Michael Meese, interview, September 6, 2011.
38. QDDR, p. 127.
39. QDDR, p. 122.
40. Condoleezza Rice, interview, August 11, 2011.
41. QDDR, p. 188.
42. QDDR, p. 189.
43. QDDR, p. 196.
44. QDDR, p. 188.
45. QDDR, p. 159.
46. Figures for "State Americans" as given in the QDDR are 1,240 in 2009 to 1,574 projected for 2012. Other U.S. government numbers rise from 623 to 1,687, while "State LES" (locally employed staff) remained the largest category of personnel and rose substantially, from 1,449 in 2009 to 2,291 in 2012. QDDR, pp. 159–160.
47. QDDR, p. 166.
48. QDDR Executive Summary, p 3.
49. At the time of this writing, influential members of the 112th Congress had just submitted a debt reduction proposal that would cut $1.3 billion of USAID's $1.6 billion in operation funds.

Chapter Five

1. Michael L. Tushman and Charles O'Reilly III, *Winning Through Innovation: A Practical Guide to Leading Organizational Change and Renewal* (Cambridge, MA: Harvard Business School Press, 1997), p. 185.
2. Ambassador Eric Edelman, interview, March 18, 2011.
3. Literally everyone interviewed for this book highlighted the analytic weakness of State's reporting.
4. Charles O'Reilly III, interview, August 22, 2011.
5. Center for Strategic and International Studies, *A Smarter, More Secure America: Report of the CSIS Commission on Smart Power*, November 6, 2007, Executive Summary, p. 7.
6. *A Foreign Affairs Budget for the Future*, p. 13.
7. *The Embassy of the Future*, p. 55.

8. U.S. Congress, Senate Select Committee on Intelligence, "Unclassified Executive Summary of the Committee Report on the Attempted Terrorist Attack on Northwest Airlines Flight 253," May 18, 2010, p. 4, http://intelligence.senate.gov/100518/1225report.pdf (viewed March 9, 2011).

9. The figure is cited in the *Embassy of the Future* report without further attribution, p. 55.

10. QDDR, pp. 163–4.

11 QDDR, pg 165.

12. *The Embassy of the Future*, p. 17.

13. QDDR, p. 173.

14. *The Embassy of the Future*, p. 11; this point was also emphasized by Ambassador Eric Edelman, interview, April 18, 2011.

15. Condoleezza Rice, interview, August 11, 2011.

16. *The Embassy of the Future*, p. 8.

17. Counter-threat training is yet another superb recommendation of the CSIS Embassy of the Future project, which it estimates would cost a pathetically small $6 million. *The Embassy of the Future*, p. 54.

18. Kosuke Takahashi, "Scandals Strain US-Japan Relations," *Asia Times*, March 8, 2011, http://www.atimes.com/atimes/Japan/MC12Dh01.html (viewed March 8, 2011).

19. Condoleezza Rice, interview, August 11, 2011.

20. Under the "Fair Share" policy, Foreign Service employees who have not served in a hardship post (15 percent differential) during the eight years prior to an upcoming transfer, must, if bidding on overseas assignments, bid on at least three posts with a differential of 15 percent or higher in two geographic regions.

21. *The Embassy of the Future*, p. 5.

22. White House sources claimed that President Obama was not more active in condemning the Libyan government's violence out of concern for the safety of American diplomats still in the country. See Helene Cooper and Mark Landler, "Obama Condemns Libya Amid Stalled Evacuation," *New York Times*, March 23, 2011, http://www.nytimes.com/2011/02/24/world/24diplomacy.html, and Ivan Watson and Joe Duran, "U.S. Diplomat Says Embassy Security 'Not the Best' in Tripoli," CNN, February 26, 2011, http://articles.cnn.com/2011-02-26/world/libya.us.diplomats_1_embassy-staff-american-diplomats-embassy-operations?_s=PM:WORLD (both viewed March 5, 2011).

23. Secretary of Defense Robert M. Gates, "Landon Lecture," Kansas State University, November 26, 2007.

24. QDDR, p. 203.
25. The State Department calculates the average cost of a domestic civil service position at $190,000, *Forging a 21st-century Diplomatic Service*, pp. 4–5.
26. QDDR, p. 199.
27. Condoleezza Rice, August 11, 2011.
28. QDDR, pp. 198–199, 195.
29. *Forging a 21st-century Diplomatic Service*, p. 17.

BIBLIOGRAPHY

American Academy of Diplomacy, American Foreign Service Association, and the Henry L. Stimson Center, *Forging a 21st-century Diplomatic Service for the United States through Professional Education and Training*, 2011.

American Academy of Diplomacy and the Henry L. Stimson Center, *A Foreign Affairs Budget for the Future: Fixing the Crisis in Diplomatic Readiness*, October 2008. http://www.stimson.org/books-reports/a-foreign-affairs-budget-for-the-future-fixing-the-crisis-in-diplomatic-readiness.

Frank Carlucci and Ian Brzezinski, *State Department Reform*, Task Force Report No. 31, sponsored by the Council on Foreign Relations and the Center for Strategic and International Studies, New York: Council on Foreign Relations Press, 2001.

Center for Strategic and International Studies, *The Embassy of the Future*, October 2007.

———, *CSIS Commission on Smart Power*, 2007.

Center for U.S. Global Engagement, *Putting 'Smart Power' to Work: An Action Agenda for the Obama Administration and the 111th Congress*, 2009.

Hillary Rodham Clinton, "Statement before the Senate Foreign Relations Committee," Nomination Hearing to be Secretary of State, Washington, DC, January 13, 2009.

———, "Foreign Policy Address at the Council on Foreign Relations," July 15, 2009.

———, "Town Hall Meeting for Employees Marking One Year at State," January 26, 2010.

James Dobbins, *Occupying Iraq: A History of the Coalition Provisional Authority*, Santa Monica, CA: RAND Corporation, 2009.

Robert M. Gates, "Landon Lecture," Kansas State University, November 26, 2007. http://www.defense.gov/speeches/speech.aspx?speechid=1199.

Government Accountability Office, *Department of State: Additional Steps Needed to Address Continuing Staffing and Experience Gaps at Hardship Posts*, GAO-09-874, September 2009.

———, *Department of State: Comprehensive Plan Needed to Address Persistent Foreign Language Shortfalls*, GAO-09-955, September 2009.

Robert Killebrew, Erin Simpson, Christopher Griffin, and Kate Bateman, *The Country Team in American Strategy*, Washington, DC: Department of State/Department of Defense, December 2006.

Kristin Lord and Richard Fontaine, *Managing 21st Century Diplomacy: Lessons from Global Corporations*, Washington, DC: Center for a New American Security, December 15, 2010.

Robert Oakley and Michael Casey Jr., *The Country Team: Restructuring America's First Line of Engagement*, Washington, DC: National Defense University Press, September 2007.

Condoleezza Rice, "Remarks at Georgetown School of Foreign Service," January 18, 2006.

Barry Rubin, *Secrets of State: The State Department and the Struggle over U.S. Foreign Policy*, New York: Oxford University Press USA, 1985.

John Schall, "Equipped for the Future: Managing U.S. Foreign Affairs in the 21st Century," Washington, DC: Henry L. Stimson Center, October 1998.

Anne-Marie Slaughter, "America's Edge: Power in the Networked Century," *Foreign Affairs*, January–February 2009.

Harry J. Thie, Roland J. Yardley, Margaret C. Harrell, and Kevin Brancato, *Alignment of Department of Defense Manpower, Resources, and Personnel Systems*, Santa Monica, CA: RAND Corporation, 2007, http://www.rand.org/pubs/technical_reports/2007/RAND_TR419.pdf.

U.S. Agency for International Development, *Corporate Learning Strategy, Office of Human Resources, Training and Education Division (CLS)*, 2009–2013, November 2009.

U.S. Congress, Senate Committee on Foreign Relations, *Embassies as Command Posts in the Anti-Terror Campaign*, Senate Report 109–52, December 2006.

U.S. Department of State, *America's Overseas Presence in the 21st Century*, Report of the Overseas Presence Advisory Council, Washington, DC: Government Printing Office, November 1999.

———, "Congressional Budget Justification," Department of State Operations, Fiscal Year 2009.

———, *Diplomatic Readiness: The Human Resources Strategy*, Washington, DC: Bureau of Human Resources, 2002.

———, *Final Report of the State Department in 2025 Working Group*, Report from the Advisory Committee on Transformational Diplomacy, Washington, DC: 2008.

———, *First Quadrennial Diplomacy and Development Review: Leading Through Civilian Power*, December 2010.

———, *Foreign Affairs Manual*, Washington, DC: Bureau of Public Affairs.

———, *Overseas Rightsizing: A Quarterly Report by the Office of Rightsizing the U.S. Government Overseas Presence, 2006/II*, Washington, DC: December 2006, http://www.state.gov/documents/organization/77386.pdf.

———, "2010 Personnel Strategy Report," prepared by Department of State's Office of Resource Management and Organizational Analysis, Washington, DC.

U.S. Foreign Service Institute, *Crisis Management Survey: Surveying the Crisis Experience of Department of State Employees Overseas*, Arlington, VA: George P. Shultz National Foreign Affairs Training Center, September 2004.

U.S. President, National Security Presidential Directive 44, "Management of Inter-agency Efforts Concerning Reconstruction and Stabilization," December 7, 2005.

ABOUT THE AUTHOR

Kori N. Schake is a research fellow at the Hoover Institution and an associate professor of international security studies at the United States Military Academy. She was educated at Stanford and the University of Maryland and previously held positions in the Pentagon, State Department, and National Security Council. Recent publications include *How to Cut a Trillion Dollars from Defense* (Orbis, winter 2012) and *Alliance in a Time of Austerity* (Centre for European Reform, January 2012). She blogs for Shadow Government at *Foreign Policy* magazine.

INDEX